Groovy Programming Language for Beginners

Your First Steps into Coding

Davis Simon

3

Discover Other Books in the Series

"Groovy Programming Language for Backend Development: Discover How Groovy Can Revolutionize Your Backend Code"

"Groovy Programming Language for Automation: Unlock the full potential of Groovy to streamline workflows, simplify coding"

"Groovy Programming language for Chatbots: The Ultimate Guide to Building Intelligent Chatbots with Ease"

"Groovy Programming Language for Data Science: Unlock the Power of Seamless Data Analysis and Automation"

"Groovy Programming Language for Web Development: Building Your First Web App"

"Groovy Programming Language for Big Data: Groovy to Build Scalable, Efficient, and Flexible Big Data Applications"

"Groovy Programming Langauge for Data Manipulation: Master the Basics and Unlock Advanced Techniques for Game-Changing Results"

"Groovy Programming Language for DevSecOps: Agile Scripting to Secure and Streamline Software Delivery With Groovy"

Disclaimer

This book, *"Groovy Programming for Beginners: Your First Steps into Coding"* by **Davis Simon**, is intended solely for educational and informational purposes. While every effort has been made to ensure the accuracy and completeness of the information provided, the author and publisher make no representations or warranties regarding its applicability, reliability, or completeness in real-world scenarios.

Readers are advised to seek professional guidance or perform their own research when applying concepts or techniques discussed in this book to specific projects, coding practices, or business decisions.

Introduction

Welcome to "**Groovy Programming Language for Beginners: Your First Steps into Coding**"! This book is tailored for individuals who are either entirely new to programming or have had some prior exposure. It aims to immerse you in the fascinating realm of Groovy, a dynamic and robust programming language that is both expressive and user-friendly.

In the current digital landscape, possessing programming skills is increasingly essential. Whether automating straightforward tasks or developing intricate applications, coding presents a multitude of opportunities. Groovy, recognized for its seamless compatibility with the Java platform, serves as an excellent starting point for newcomers. It enables you to write concise and comprehensible code while taking advantage of the extensive array of Java libraries and frameworks.

This book will guide you through a journey that clarifies programming principles and introduces you to the core aspects of Groovy. You will cultivate a programmer's mindset, enhance your problem-solving abilities, and acquire practical experience through interactive coding exercises. Each chapter is designed to build upon the last, ensuring a gradual advancement from fundamental syntax to the creation of your own simple applications.

Here is what you can anticipate in this book:

Fundamental Concepts: We will explore the foundational elements of programming, including variables, data types, control structures, and functions, establishing a robust base for your learning.

Groovy Syntax and Features: You will uncover the distinctive attributes of Groovy, such as its straightforward syntax and powerful natural language capabilities, making coding not only accessible but also enjoyable.

Hands-On Projects: Throughout the text, you will participate in practical projects aimed at reinforcing your understanding, enabling you to apply the concepts learned and witness your progress in real-time.

Resources for Further Learning: As you complete this book, you'll find guidance on how to continue your programming journey, suggesting further resources and communities to help you grow.

Chapter 1: Introduction to Groovy Programming

Groovy is a robust programming language that offers optional typing and operates on the Java Virtual Machine (JVM). It is crafted to complement Java, equipping developers with a rich syntax and dynamic features while ensuring complete compatibility with Java code. In recent years, Groovy has gained significant traction, particularly in web development, scripting, and testing frameworks, owing to its ease of use and adaptability.

The Origins of Groovy

Groovy was developed in 2003 by James Strachan, with the intention of merging the advantageous aspects of dynamic languages like Python and Ruby with the established structure of Java. Fundamentally, Groovy enhances the Java programming language by introducing additional functionalities, enabling developers to create robust applications with reduced boilerplate code. Over time, Groovy has evolved into a multifaceted language utilized across various fields, including web development—especially with the Grails web framework—scripting for automating build processes through tools like Apache Ant, and in testing frameworks such as Spock.

Key Features of Groovy

Dynamic Typing: While Java is statically typed, Groovy allows developers to create dynamic types, offering greater flexibility and reducing verbosity in code. You can declare variables without explicitly specifying their types.

Syntactic Sugar: Groovy simplifies the syntax for common programming tasks. For instance, the use of closures (anonymous blocks of code) in Groovy makes writing iterative and functional-style code much more natural.

Optional Semicolons: Unlike Java, where semicolons are mandatory to terminate statements, Groovy allows developers to omit them, resulting in cleaner and more readable code.

String Interpolation: Groovy introduces string interpolation, making it easy to embed expressions directly within string literals. This improves code readability and reduces the need for explicit string concatenation.

Native Collections: Groovy features built-in support for lists, maps, and ranges using a more convenient syntax compared to Java, making it easier to manage data collections.

Metaprogramming Capabilities: Groovy supports dynamic method and property additions, allowing developers to modify classes at runtime, which can facilitate the development of more flexible libraries and frameworks.

Groovy and Java Interoperability

One of Groovy's most significant advantages is its seamless integration with Java. Groovy code can directly call Java libraries, and vice versa, creating a robust environment for hybrid projects. Developers can leverage existing Java frameworks and libraries, ensuring that Groovy can be adopted incrementally. This interoperability means that developers can start using Groovy for specific tasks within a larger Java application without needing to rewrite everything.

The Groovy Ecosystem

The Groovy ecosystem is rich with tools and libraries designed to enhance development:

Grails: An integrated web application framework built on Groovy, which follows the "convention over configuration" principle, allowing developers to get applications up and running quickly.

Spock: A testing and specification framework for Java and Groovy applications, known for its expressive syntax and powerful features.

Gradle: A build automation tool that utilizes Groovy to define build configurations, offering a flexible and powerful way to handle projects.

When to Use Groovy

Groovy is particularly well-suited for:

Rapid Prototyping: Its expressive syntax and dynamic typing facilitate quick and efficient prototype development.

Scripting Tasks: Groovy is an excellent choice for scripting in the JVM ecosystem, including automation and build processes.

Web Applications: With frameworks like Grails, Groovy provides a powerful environment for developing robust web applications efficiently.

Testing: The Spock framework, built on Groovy, offers an expressive and powerful way to write tests, making it easy to implement test-driven development (TDD) practices.

With its dynamic features, expressive syntax, and seamless interoperability with Java, Groovy has carved out a crucial niche in modern software development. As we continue through this book, we will explore the foundational aspects of Groovy programming, offering practical examples and applications to help you harness the power of Groovy in your projects. Thus, embarking on your Groovy journey sets the stage for innovative and productive programming experiences.

The Power of Groovy for Programming

In the evolving landscape of programming languages, Groovy stands out as a powerful, flexible, and innovative option for developers seeking to enhance productivity while writing cleaner and more expressive code. Originally created for the Java platform, Groovy is an agile language that combines the best features of both Python and Java, which empowers developers to produce robust applications with ease. This chapter explores the capabilities, advantages, and use cases of Groovy in programming, demonstrating why it has become a popular choice among developers in various fields.

Understanding Groovy: A Brief Overview

Groovy is an object-oriented programming language that integrates seamlessly with the Java ecosystem. It is dynamically typed, which means developers can write code without declaring data types, allowing for faster development cycles. Groovy is not merely a replacement for Java; rather, it serves as a complement, adding syntactic sugar and simplifying complex tasks. With a focus on developer productivity, Groovy offers features such as closures, dynamic typing, and a powerful syntax that makes everyday coding tasks easier and more intuitive.

Key Features of Groovy

Syntax Simplicity: Groovy's syntax is concise and expressive. Unlike Java, Groovy does not require semicolons or explicit getters and setters, making the code more readable. For example, what would take several lines in Java can often be accomplished in just a single line in Groovy.

Dynamic Typing: Groovy supports dynamic typing and metaprogramming, allowing developers to write more flexible code. Variables can change type at runtime, making the language highly adaptable and suitable for rapid iteration.

Closures: Groovy introduced closures, which are first-class objects capable of encapsulating functionality. This feature allows developers to write more reusable and modular code, leading to better- organized applications. Closures are especially useful in functional programming paradigms and event- driven systems.

Grails Framework: One of the most significant contributions of Groovy to the programming world is the Grails framework, which facilitates rapid application development. It follows the "convention over configuration" principle, allowing developers to focus on building applications rather than dealing with boilerplate configuration.

Integration with Java: Groovy is fully interoperable with Java, allowing developers to leverage existing Java libraries seamlessly. This compatibility makes it easier to integrate Groovy into existing Java projects, enhancing their functionality without the challenge of rewriting code.

Advantages of Using Groovy

Rapid Development: The flexibility and simplicity of Groovy significantly reduce development time. The language's intuitive syntax allows developers to prototype and iterate quickly, making it an excellent choice for startups and agile teams.

Increased Productivity: Groovy's features, such as robust error handling and concise code structure, lead to fewer bugs and faster debugging processes. This increased productivity translates into shorter release cycles and more efficient projects.

Active Community and Ecosystem: Groovy boasts a passionate community that contributes to its growth and provides extensive libraries, plugins, and frameworks. The availability of resources and support makes embracing Groovy less daunting for new developers.

Versatile Use Cases: Groovy is suitable for various applications, from build automation (with Gradle) to server-side web development (with Grails). It can also be used for scripting, testing, and even in domain- specific language (DSL) creation, showcasing its versatility.

Real-World Applications of Groovy

Groovy has been adopted by numerous organizations across various sectors. Here are a few notable applications:

Web Development: Companies such as Netflix and

LinkedIn utilize Groovy and Grails for their web applications. The ability to create scalable, high-performance applications quickly has made Groovy a preferred choice in the tech industry.

Build Automation: Gradle, the powerful build automation tool used in many Java projects, is primarily written in Groovy. This tool allows developers to manage dependencies, build processes, and deployment efficiently.

Testing: Groovy is widely used for automated testing frameworks, such as Spock, which is designed for enterprise-grade testing. Spock's expressive syntax makes writing tests easier and more maintainable.

Challenges and Considerations

Despite its strengths, Groovy is not without challenges. Developers coming from a strict Java background may find it difficult to adjust to dynamic typing and the absence of certain Java conventions. Additionally, while Groovy code can be more succinct, the lack of explicit type declarations may lead to less clarity in larger codebases if not managed properly.

The power of Groovy lies in its ability to enhance productivity, facilitate rapid development, and simplify the coding experience. With its dynamic features and seamless integration with the Java ecosystem, Groovy continues to empower developers, enabling them to create high-quality applications with ease. As the demand for agile and efficient programming languages grows, Groovy stands poised to play an integral role in shaping the future of development across industries, making it an essential language for any modern programmer's toolkit.

Setting Up Your Development Environment

Groovy is an agile, dynamic language for the Java platform that enables developers to write code more efficiently and intuitively. It boasts a range of features, including syntactic sugar for seamless Java integration, support for domain-specific languages (DSLs), and capabilities such as closures, dynamic typing, and operator overloading. Setting up a development environment efficiently will empower you to leverage Groovy's full potential in building applications that are robust and maintainable.

In this chapter, we will walk through the necessary steps to set up your Groovy development environment. We will cover the installation of Groovy, integrated development environments (IDEs), and additional tools that enhance the development experience. By the end, you will have a fully functional environment to start coding in Groovy.

Prerequisites

Before diving into the setup process, ensure your system meets the following prerequisites:

Java Development Kit (JDK): Groovy runs on the Java Virtual Machine (JVM), thus you will need to have a JDK installed. Groovy is compatible with JDK 8 and above. It is recommended to use the latest Long Term Support (LTS) version of JDK.

Basic Command Line Knowledge: Familiarity with the command line is necessary for the installation of tools and running scripts.

Step 1: Installing the Java Development Kit (JDK)

Download the JDK:

Visit the [Oracle JDK downloads page](https://www.oracle.com/java/technologies/javase-downloads.html) (or adopt OpenJDK from [Adoptium](https://adoptium.net/)).

Choose the version suitable for your operating system, download the installer, and follow the installation instructions.

Set Up Environment Variables:

Windows:

Go to "System Properties" "Environment Variables" and add a new system variable named

`JAVA_HOME` pointing to your JDK installation directory (e.g., `C:\Program Files\Java\jdk-11`).

Append `%JAVA_HOME%\bin` to the `Path` variable.

macOS/Linux:

Open your terminal and add the following lines to your `~/.bash_profile` or `~/.bashrc` file:

```bash
export JAVA_HOME=/Library/Java/JavaVirtualMachines/jdk-11.jdk/Contents/Home    # macOS export JAVA_HOME=/usr/lib/jvm/java-11-openjdk-amd64    # Linux

export PATH=$JAVA_HOME/bin:$PATH
```

```
```

Run `source ~/.bash_profile` or `source ~/.bashrc` to apply changes.

Verify Installation:

Run the command `java -version` in your terminal/command prompt to verify the JDK installation.
Step 2: Installing Groovy

Once JDK is installed, you can proceed to install Groovy. There are several methods to do this:

Option A: Using SDKMAN!

SDKMAN! is a popular tool for managing parallel versions of multiple Software Development Kits. It's a simple way to install, switch, and manage Groovy versions.

Install SDKMAN!:

Open your terminal and run the following command:

```bash
curl -s "https://get.sdkman.io" | bash
```

- Follow the instructions that appear after the installation. Restart your terminal or run `source "$HOME/.sdkman/bin/sdkman-init.sh"`.

Install Groovy via SDKMAN!:

In your terminal, type:

```bash
sdk install groovy
```

Verify Groovy Installation:

Run the command `groovy -version` to check if Groovy is installed correctly. ### Option B: Downloading from the Groovy Website

Download Groovy:

Visit the [Apache Groovy downloads page](https://groovy.apache.org/download.html) and download the latest distribution.

Extract the Files:

Unzip the downloaded file to your desired location.

Set Up Environment Variables:

Similar to setting up the JDK, set the `GROOVY_HOME` environment variable pointing to your Groovy installation:

```bash
export GROOVY_HOME=/path/to/groovy export PATH=$GROOVY_HOME/bin:$PATH
```

Make sure to apply these changes by sourcing the file as mentioned earlier.

Verify Groovy Installation:

Again, use `groovy -version` to confirm that Groovy is functioning properly. ## Step 3: Choosing an Integrated Development Environment (IDE)

An effective IDE can significantly improve your productivity. Here are some popular options for Groovy development:

IntelliJ IDEA

Download and Install IntelliJ IDEA:

Visit the [IntelliJ IDEA download page](https://www.jetbrains.com/idea/download/) and download the Community Edition (or Ultimate if you require advanced features).

Follow the installation instructions.

Create a New Groovy Project:

Open IntelliJ IDEA, and select "New Project."

Choose "Groovy" from the project types and set your JDK and Groovy SDK. ### Eclipse with Groovy Plugin

Download and Install Eclipse IDE:

Visit the [Eclipse downloads page](https://www.eclipse.org/downloads/) and download the IDE for Java Developers.

Install Groovy Plugin:

Once Eclipse is installed, go to "Help" "Eclipse Marketplace."

Search for the "Groovy Development Tools" plugin and install it.

Create a New Groovy Project:

Select "File" "New" "Other," then choose "Groovy" and "Groovy Project." ### Visual Studio Code

Download Visual Studio Code:

Visit the [VS Code download page](https://code.visualstudio.com/) and download the installer.

Install Groovy Extension:

Open VS Code and navigate to the Extensions view by clicking on the square icon in the sidebar.

Search for "Groovy" and install the appropriate extension for Groovy support.

Create a New Groovy File:

Create a new file with the `.groovy` extension and start writing your Groovy code. ## Step 4: Testing Your Setup

Before you begin your development journey, it is a good idea to verify that everything is working properly.

Open Your IDE: Start the IDE you have chosen.

Create a New Groovy File: In your new project, create a file named `HelloWorld.groovy`.

Write Sample Code:

```groovy
println 'Hello, World!'
```

Run the Code:

- Use the IDE's run/debug options to execute your Groovy script. You should see "Hello, World!" printed to the console, indicating that your development environment is set up correctly.

In the following chapters, we will explore Groovy features, syntax, and various programming constructs to enhance your skills and significantly improve your productivity as a developer. Happy coding!

Chapter 2: Getting Started with Groovy

Groovy is an agile and dynamic language for the Java platform that simplifies and enhances programming in Java. It's an object-oriented language with a syntax that is familiar to Java developers, yet it introduces powerful and expressive features that make it a joy to work with. In this chapter, we will guide you through the essentials of getting started with Groovy, including installation, setting up your development environment, and writing your first Groovy program.

2.1 Installing Groovy

Before you can start exploring the features of Groovy, you need to have it installed on your system. Groovy can be easily installed in various ways depending on your operating system.

2.1.1 Installation on Windows

Download Groovy: Visit the official Apache Groovy website (groovy.apache.org) and download the binary distribution.

Unzip the Archive: Extract the downloaded ZIP file to a directory of your choice.

Set Environment Variables:

Right-click on 'This PC' and select 'Properties.'

Click on 'Advanced system settings' and then on 'Environment Variables.'

Under 'System variables,' click on 'New' and add:

Variable name: `GROOVY_HOME`

Variable value: The path to the directory where you unpacked Groovy.

Find the `Path` variable in the System variables section and click 'Edit.' Add the following:

`%GROOVY_HOME%\bin`

Verify Installation: Open a Command Prompt and type `groovy --version`. If installed correctly, you should see the Groovy version printed in the console.

2.1.2 Installation on macOS

Using Homebrew: If you have Homebrew installed, you can install Groovy easily by running:

```bash
brew install groovy
```

Verification: After installation, check if Groovy is installed by executing:

```bash
groovy --version
```

2.1.3 Installation on Linux

Using SDKMAN!: SDKMAN! is a tool for managing parallel versions of multiple Software Development Kits on most Unix-based systems. Install it by running:

```bash
curl -s https://get.sdkman.io | bash
source "$HOME/.sdkman/bin/sdkman-init.sh"
```

```
```

Then, install Groovy with:

```bash
sdk install groovy
```

Verification: Check your installation using:

```bash
groovy --version
```

2.2 Setting Up Your Development Environment

Once Groovy is installed, you can choose your development environment. While you can use any text editor, integrated development environments (IDEs) enhance productivity by providing features such as syntax highlighting, debugging tools, and more. Some popular options include:

IntelliJ IDEA: Offers excellent support for Groovy and provides many features that enhance development.

Eclipse with Groovy Plugin: Eclipse can be enhanced with the Groovy Development Tools (GDT) to create a full-fledged Groovy development environment.

Visual Studio Code: With the right extensions, you can enjoy Groovy syntax highlighting and more in VS Code.

2.2.1 Creating Your First Groovy Script

Now that you have your environment set up, let's write

your first Groovy script.

Open your preferred text editor or IDE.

Create a new file named `HelloWorld.groovy`.

Add the following code to the file:

```groovy
println 'Hello, World!'
```

Save the file.

2.2.2 Running Your Groovy Script

To run your Groovy script, open a terminal or command prompt and navigate to the directory where your

`HelloWorld.groovy` file resides. Execute the following command:

```bash
groovy HelloWorld.groovy
```

If all goes well, you should see the output:

```
Hello, World!
```

2.3 Understanding Groovy Syntax

Groovy's syntax is designed to be intuitive and less verbose than Java. Here are some key features to help you understand Groovy syntax better:

2.3.1 Dynamic Typing

Groovy uses dynamic typing, which means you don't have to explicitly declare types for variables. For instance:

```groovy
def name = "John" def age = 30
```

The `def` keyword allows you to declare variables without specifying their type. ### 2.3.2 String Interpolation

You can easily include variables within strings using the GString syntax (using double quotes). For example:

```groovy
def name = "John"
println "Hello, ${name}!"
```

This will output:

```
Hello, John!
```

2.3.3 Closures

Closures are one of Groovy's most powerful features. They are similar to anonymous functions in other programming languages. Here's a simple example:

```groovy
def square = { int number -> number * number } println
```

27

```
square(5) // Output: 25
` ` `
```

In this chapter, you also got a glimpse of Groovy's syntax and features, such as dynamic typing and closures. As you continue to explore Groovy, you'll uncover many more powerful features that can significantly enhance your coding experience.

In the following chapters, we will dive deeper into Groovy's capabilities, including working with collections, integrating with Java, and building robust applications. Let's continue our journey into the world of Groovy!

Writing Your First Groovy Script

Groovy is an agile and dynamic language for the Java platform. It builds upon the strengths of Java but provides developers with a much more succinct and expressive syntax. Groovy is designed to be simple for Java developers to pick up, while still being powerful enough to handle more complex scripting tasks.

Whether you're new to programming or an experienced Java developer, Groovy offers a friendly entry point into scripting.

Setting Up Your Environment

Before you can start writing Groovy scripts, you'll need to ensure that you have the proper environment in place. Here's how to get started:

Install Java Development Kit (JDK): Make sure you

have the JDK installed on your system, preferably the latest version. You can download it from [Oracle's website](https://www.oracle.com/java/technologies/javase-downloads.html) or choose an open-source alternative like OpenJDK.

Install Groovy: You have several options for installing Groovy:

Using SDKMAN: This is a popular tool to manage parallel versions of multiple Software Development Kits on most Unix-based systems. Install SDKMAN and then run `sdk install groovy`.

Using Homebrew (macOS): Run `brew install groovy` to install it.

Direct ZIP Distribution: You can download Groovy from the [official Groovy website](https://groovy-lang.org/download.html) and follow the setup instructions.

Verify Your Installation: To verify that Groovy is correctly installed, open your terminal or command prompt and type:

```bash

groovy --version

```

You should see the version of Groovy displayed. If you see a message stating that the command is not found, revisit the installation steps.

Your First Groovy Script

Now that we have the environment set up, it's time to

write your first Groovy script. We'll create a simple script that outputs a greeting message to the console.

Create a New File: Open your favorite text editor and create a new file named `HelloWorld.groovy`. You can use any text editor like Visual Studio Code, Notepad++, or even the built-in Notepad.

Write Your Script: Type the following code into your `HelloWorld.groovy` file:

```groovy
// HelloWorld.groovy println 'Hello, World!'
```

In this script:

The `//` denotes a comment in Groovy, which can help document your code.

The `println` method is used to print text to the console, and the string `'Hello, World!'` is what will be displayed.

Save Your File: Make sure to save your changes before proceeding to the next step. ### Running Your Script

To run your Groovy script, you need to execute it from the command line:

Open Your Terminal or Command Prompt: Navigate to the directory where you saved your

`HelloWorld.groovy` file.

Run the Script: Enter the following command:

```bash
groovy HelloWorld.groovy
```

```
```

If everything is set up correctly, you should see the output:

```
```

Hello, World!

```
```

Understanding the Output

Congratulations! You've just executed your first Groovy script. Here's a brief breakdown of your code and execution flow:

Script Structure: This simple program consists of a single line that calls the `println` method. In Groovy, you can write much more complex scripts, but this example showcases the simplicity of the language.

Dynamic Typing: Unlike Java, Groovy is dynamically typed, which means you don't need to declare variable types explicitly. This reduces boilerplate code and allows for quicker development.

Interactivity: You can modify and rerun your script to see different outputs. As you learn more about Groovy, you'll discover how to take user inputs, handle conditions, and implement loops.

Next Steps

Having successfully written and executed your first Groovy script, it's time to explore further. Here are some suggested next steps:

Experiment: Modify your script to print different messages or perform basic arithmetic operations.

Learn Groovy Syntax: Get familiar with lists, maps, closures, and other Groovy features that make it powerful and easy to use.

Explore Groovy's Integrations: Discover how Groovy can be integrated with Java classes and libraries, enabling you to leverage existing Java code effectively.

Writing your first Groovy script is a gateway to understanding and utilizing the power of Groovy as a scripting language on the Java platform. From simple print statements to complex logic, Groovy offers a wide array of features that can streamline your development process. As you continue to explore Groovy, you'll find it a valuable addition to your programming toolkit. Happy scripting!

Basic Syntax and Structure in Groovy

Directly integrating with existing Java code, Groovy allows developers to leverage the full capabilities of the Java ecosystem while benefiting from Groovy's concise syntax and features that simplify common tasks. In this chapter, we will explore the basic syntax and structure of Groovy, including variables, data types, control structures, and the essential building blocks of Groovy programming.

1. Understanding Variables

In Groovy, variables are defined using the `def` keyword, although it is optional, allowing for a more concise syntax. The type of a variable is inferred during the assignment, making Groovy a dynamically typed language.

```groovy
def name = "John Doe" // String
age = 28       // Integer, inferred type
```

Groovy also supports defining variables with type annotations. This can help improve code readability and clarity, especially for complex systems.

```groovy
String name = "John Doe" int age = 28
```

Variables can be reassigned, and their types can change dynamically, reflecting Groovy's flexibility.

```groovy
age = "Twenty-Eight" // Now age is a String
```

2. Data Types

Groovy includes several built-in data types that are similar to Java's, such as:

Primitive Types: `int`, `double`, `boolean`, `char`, etc.

Reference Types: Objects and Collections, like `String`, `List`, and `Map`.

Groovy provides additional data types such as lists and maps that allow for quick and efficient data handling. ### Lists

Lists in Groovy are created using square brackets `[]`.

They can hold any type of objects and are mutable.

```groovy
def fruits = ['Apple', 'Banana', 'Cherry']
fruits.add('Durian') // Adding an element

println(fruits)      // Output: [Apple, Banana, Cherry, Durian]
```

Maps

Maps are key-value pairs created using the syntax `[:]`. They are also mutable and can hold a variety of object types.

```groovy
def person = [name: 'John', age: 28]

person.location = 'New York' // Adding a new key-value pair println(person) // Output: [name:John, age:28, location:New York]
```

3. Control Structures

Groovy supports the standard control structures familiar to Java developers, including conditional statements and loops.

Conditional Statements

The basic `if` statement operates similarly to Java but can also support a more concise syntax using the Groovy truth.

```groovy
```

```groovy
def score = 85
if (score >= 90) { println("Grade: A")
} else if (score >= 80) { println("Grade: B")
} else { println("Grade: C")
}
```

Switch Statement

Switch statements in Groovy can evaluate different types, including strings, integers, and even lists.

```groovy
def day = "Monday"
switch (day) { case "Monday":
println("Start of the week!") break
case "Friday":
println("End of the week!") break
default:
println("It's just another day.")
}
```

Loops

Groovy supports traditional for and while loops, but it also offers the `each` method for enhanced iteration, particularly with collections.

```groovy
def numbers = [1, 2, 3, 4, 5]
// Traditional loop
for (int i = 0; i < numbers.size(); i++) {
println(numbers[i])
}
// Using `each` numbers.each { number->
println(number)
}
```

4. Methods

Defining methods in Groovy is straightforward and supports optional return types. Methods can also have optional parameters with default values.

```groovy
def greet(String name = 'Guest') { return "Hello, ${name}!"
}
println(greet())    // Output: Hello, Guest!
println(greet('John'))  // Output: Hello, John!
```

5. Exception Handling

Groovy uses a familiar try-catch mechanism for exception handling. Additionally, it has built-in support for the `@Grab` annotation, which allows for easy dependency management.

```groovy
groovy try {
def result = 100 / 0
} catch (ArithmeticException e) { println("Division by zero is not allowed!")
}
```

Groovy's basic syntax and structure make it an inviting choice for developers looking to leverage the flexibility of scripting while maintaining the robustness of Java. This chapter has introduced you to the essential components of Groovy, including variables, data types, control structures, methods, and exception handling. By understanding these basics, you are now ready to delve deeper into the more advanced features and capabilities of Groovy, paving the way for building efficient and elegant applications.

Chapter 3: Variables and Data Types

This chapter will delve into the crucial concepts of variables and data types in Groovy, a versatile programming language that combines the powers of both scripting and traditional object-oriented programming. This chapter will provide you with a comprehensive understanding of how to declare and manipulate variables, as well as the various data types Groovy supports.

3.1 What are Variables?

At its core, a variable can be seen as a named storage location in memory that holds data which may change during the execution of a program. Assigning a value to a variable allows you to easily reference and manipulate that value throughout your code. In Groovy, variables can be created without a strict declaration of their data types, thanks to its dynamic typing feature, which infers the variable's type at runtime based on the assigned value.

3.1.1 Declaring Variables

In Groovy, declaring a variable is a straightforward process. You can declare a variable using the `def` keyword, which tells the Groovy compiler to create a variable without specifying the type explicitly:

```groovy
def message = "Hello, Groovy!"
```

Here, `message` is a variable holding a string value. The compiler infers that `message` is a string without needing an explicit type declaration.

You can also declare variables with specific data types when you want to increase code clarity or enforce certain programming conventions:

```groovy
String greeting = "Welcome to Groovy!" int count = 10

double price = 99.99
```

In the above examples, we have specifically declared `greeting` as a String, `count` as an Integer, and `price` as a Double.

3.1.2 Variable Scope

Variable scope determines the accessibility of a variable within different parts of your program. Groovy supports three primary types of variable scopes: local, instance, and class variables.

- **Local Variables** are declared within a method, closure, or block, and are only accessible within that scope.

```groovy
def myMethod() {

def localVar = "I'm local" println(localVar) // Accessible here

}

println(localVar) // Throws an error: Cannot find 'localVar'
```

- **Instance Variables** are declared within a class and

39

are tied to instances of that class. Each object of the class has its own copy.

```groovy
class MyClass {
def instanceVar = "I'm an instance variable"

def show() {
println(instanceVar) // Accessible here
}
}
```

- **Class Variables** are declared with the `static` keyword, shared among all instances of the class.

```groovy
class MyClass {
static def classVar = "I'm a class variable"

static void show() {
println(classVar) // Accessible here
}
}
```

3.2 Data Types in Groovy

Data types are essential as they define the nature of the

data that can be stored in a variable. Groovy is highly flexible and supports both primitive and complex data types.

3.2.1 Primitive Data Types

Groovy provides several primitive data types, which correspond to the basic types in Java:

Integer: Represents whole numbers.

Double: Represents decimal numbers (floating point).

Boolean: Represents true or false values.

Character: Represents single characters, although it's less commonly used directly in Groovy.

Byte: Represents an 8-bit signed integer.

Short: Represents a 16-bit signed integer.

Long: Represents a 64-bit signed integer. Example of declaring primitive data types:

```groovy
int age = 25

double temperature = 36.6 boolean isGroovyFun = true
```

3.2.2 Complex Data Types

In addition to primitive types, Groovy has a rich set of complex data types which include:

Strings: Groovy has excellent support for strings, including multi-line strings defined with three double quotes (`"""`).

```groovy
```

```groovy
String multiline = """This is a multi-line
string in Groovy."""
```

Lists: Groovy provides robust list capabilities, allowing for dynamic and mutable collections of ordered items.

```groovy
def colors = ["Red", "Green", "Blue"]
```

Maps: A key-value pair collection that allows you to access elements via a unique key.

```groovy
def person = [name: "John", age: 30, hasCar: true]
```

3.2.3 Type Conversion

Groovy supports implicit and explicit type conversion. Implicit conversion happens automatically, while explicit conversion needs to be specified by the programmer.

Example of implicit conversion:

```groovy
def num = 10  // num is inferred as Integer def decimal = 20.5
// Implicit conversion during addition
def sum = num + decimal // sum is inferred as Double
```

Example of explicit conversion:

```groovy
def stringToInt = "123"

def intValue = stringToInt.toInteger()  // Converts string to Integer
```

Understanding variables and data types in Groovy is essential for effective programming in this language. The dynamic typing capability offers flexibility while still allowing for robust data management through both primitive and complex types. As we continue to explore Groovy, keep these concepts in mind to develop clean, efficient, and readable code. In the next chapter, we will delve into control structures, allowing you to make decisions and execute code conditionally.

Declaring Variables in Groovy

One of the fundamental aspects of programming in Groovy is understanding how to declare and use variables. In this chapter, we will explore the various ways to declare variables in Groovy, along with best practices and examples to effectively illustrate these concepts.

1. Understanding Variables

In programming, a variable is a symbolic name associated with a value and whose associated value may change. Variables serve as containers for data, allowing developers to store, modify, and retrieve information throughout a program. In Groovy, variable declaration is designed to be simple and intuitive.

2. Variable Declaration Syntax

Groovy allows for a concise and flexible syntax when declaring variables. Here are the primary ways to declare variables:

2.1. Using `def`

The most common way to declare a variable in Groovy is by using the `def` keyword, which signifies that you are creating a new variable without specifying its type. This leads to dynamic typing, which is one of Groovy's key features.

```groovy
def name = "John Doe" def age = 30
def isActive = true
```

In this example, `name` is a string, `age` is an integer, and `isActive` is a boolean. The `def` keyword allows any type of data to be assigned to the variable.

2.2. Using Explicit Types

While using `def` is convenient, you can also explicitly declare the type of a variable if desired. This provides clarity about the expected data type.

```groovy
String name = "Jane Doe" int age = 25
boolean isActive = false
```

```
```

Declaring the type of the variable enhances the readability of the code and can facilitate debugging by ensuring that certain operations are only performed on the appropriate data types.

2.3. Type Inference

Groovy supports type inference, which means you can avoid explicitly declaring the type while still being type-safe. The following example demonstrates this feature:

```groovy
var number = 100 // Declares an Integer

var message = "Hello, Groovy!" // Declares a String
```

In this context, `var` is a new addition introduced in more recent versions of Groovy, making it easier for developers to define variables without cluttering their code with type declarations.

3. Variable Scope

The scope of a variable determines where it can be accessed within your code. There are two main types of variable scope in Groovy:

3.1. Local Variables

Local variables are declared within a method or a block and can only be accessed within that method or block.

```groovy
def greet(name) {
```

```
def greeting = "Hello, ${name}" return greeting
}
println(greet("Alice")) // Output: Hello, Alice
// println(greeting) // This would cause an error because
`greeting` is not accessible outside of the greet method.
```

3.2. Instance and Class Variables

Variables declared at the class level are known as instance variables (if they are declared within a class but outside any method), and they can be accessed by all methods within that class.

```groovy
class Person {
String name int age
def displayDetails() {
println("Name: ${name}, Age: ${age}")
}
}
def person = new Person(name: "Bob", age: 25)
person.displayDetails() // Output: Name: Bob, Age: 25
```

In this example, `name` and `age` are instance variables accessible inside `displayDetails()`. ## 4. Immutable and Mutable Variables

Groovy provides the ability to define variables that are immutable (cannot be changed after they are initialized) by using the `final` keyword.

```groovy
final int constantValue = 100

// constantValue = 200 // This would raise an error since
constantValue is immutable.
```

In contrast, regular variables can be mutable, allowing for their values to change throughout the program. ## 5. Best Practices for Variable Declaration

Use `def` for Simplicity: Use `def` when you do not need strict type checking. It keeps your code clean and concise.

Clarify with Explicit Types: When necessary, use explicit types for better code readability, especially in public/interface methods.

Follow Naming Conventions: Utilize meaningful variable names to enhance code clarity. Stick to camelCase for variable naming, e.g., `firstName`, `accountBalance`.

Limit Scope: Keep variables as local as possible to reduce complexity and enhance maintainability.

Use Immutables When Appropriate: Use `final` when you want to ensure that a variable's value should not change after initialization.

Declaring variables in Groovy is straightforward and flexible, allowing developers to create readable and maintainable code. By understanding how to effectively declare and manage variable scope, as well as making sound choices between mutable and immutable variables, Groovy developers can write clear and efficient programs. As you continue learning Groovy, remember that effective variable declaration is fundamental to crafting well-structued applications.

Understanding Data Types in Groovy

Groovy, a powerful and agile scripting language for the Java platform, is often praised for its concise syntax and dynamic capabilities. Yet, as with any programming language, understanding its data types is fundamental to harnessing its full potential. In this chapter, we will delve into the primary data types available in Groovy, how they differ from one another, and how they can be utilized effectively in your Groovy applications.

1. Primitive Data Types

Groovy inherits its primitive data types from Java, but it offers enhanced flexibility by treating them as objects. Here are the primary primitive data types:

1.1 Integer

In Groovy, integers can be defined simply by assigning a whole number to a variable.

```groovy
def age = 25
```

This variable can hold any integer value, and because of Groovy's dynamic nature, you can change its type at runtime without any compilation issues.

1.2 Float and Double

Floating-point numbers are defined using decimal points. In Groovy, you can define float and double with the following syntax:

```groovy
def price = 19.99f  // Float
def distance = 1234.56 // Double
```

Floats in Groovy are represented with the 'f' suffix, while doubles are treated as the default floating point. ### 1.3 Boolean

Boolean data types are quite straightforward in Groovy, holding one of two values: `true` or `false`.

```groovy
def isAvailable = true
```

These values can be used in control structures like `if` statements or loops. ## 2. String Data Type

Strings in Groovy are a collection of characters and can be defined in multiple ways: single quotes, double quotes, or triple quotes.

2.1 Single and Double Quotes

Single quotes represent static strings, while double quotes allow for GString expressions:

```groovy
def name = 'John Doe' // Single quotes
def greeting = "Hello, $name!" // GString with variable
```

interpolation
```

```

2.2 Multi-line Strings

Triple quotes allow for multi-line strings, preserving line breaks:

```groovy
def multiLineString = """

This is a string that spans multiple lines."""
```

3. Collection Data Types

Collections are essential in Groovy for managing groups of objects. The language provides several built-in options:

3.1 Lists

Lists can be created using square brackets. They are ordered and can hold duplicates:

```groovy
def fruits = ['apple', 'banana', 'orange']
```

You can manipulate lists using various methods such as adding, removing, or sorting elements. ### 3.2 Maps

A map is a collection of key-value pairs. Maps can be defined using colons to separate keys from values:

```groovy
def person = [name: 'Alice', age: 30]
```

You can access the values by their keys, which makes maps incredibly useful for handling structured data. ### 3.3 Sets

Sets are collections that do not allow duplicates. They can be created using the `as Set` syntax:

```groovy
def uniqueFruits = ['apple', 'banana', 'apple'] as Set
```

This collection will automatically filter out duplicate entries.

4. Custom and Complex Data Types

In addition to the built-in data types, Groovy allows developers to define their own complex types using classes.

4.1 Creating a Class

You can create custom data types by defining a class, encapsulating properties and behaviors:

```groovy
class Person {
String name int age

String introduce() {
return "Hi, I'm $name and I'm $age years old."
}
}
def bob = new Person(name: 'Bob', age: 28) println bob.introduce()
```

```
` ` `
```

This flexibility makes Groovy a powerful language for creating object-oriented applications. ## 5. Type Inference and Dynamic Typing

One of Groovy's strengths lies in its dynamic typing system. You don't have to declare the type of a variable explicitly, as the compiler infers it at runtime. This makes your code cleaner and more readable:

```groovy
def message = "Welcome to Groovy!"
```

However, if you prefer static type checking or are working in larger applications where types matter for readability and maintainability, you can use type annotations.

```groovy
String message = "Welcome to Groovy!"
```

Understanding data types in Groovy is crucial for effective programming. From primitive types to complex objects, the flexibility and dynamic nature of Groovy's type system allows developers to create elegant solutions quickly. In this chapter, we explored the fundamental data types, collection types, and the capabilities of custom classes in Groovy. As you continue your journey through Groovy, remember that mastering these concepts will serve as a strong foundation for building robust and efficient applications.

Chapter 4: Operators and Expressions

They allow us to manipulate data, control program flow, and perform calculations. In Groovy, operators are not only versatile but also enriched with syntactic sugar that makes tasks simpler and more intuitive. This chapter will explore various operators in Groovy, detailing how they work, the types available, and examples demonstrating their use.

4.1 Types of Operators

Groovy provides a rich set of operators, categorized as follows:

4.1.1 Arithmetic Operators

Arithmetic operators are used for basic mathematical calculations. Groovy supports the standard arithmetic operators:

- **Addition (`+`)**

Subtraction (`-`)

Multiplication (`*`)

- **Division (`/`)**

- **Modulus (`%`)**

Example:

```groovy
def a = 10 def b = 3

println a + b // Outputs: 13 println a - b // Outputs: 7
println a * b // Outputs: 30 println a / b // Outputs:
3.33333 println a % b // Outputs: 1
```

4.1.2 Relational Operators

Relational operators are used to compare two values. They return a Boolean value indicating whether the relation holds true.

- **Equal to (`==`)**

Not equal to (`!=`)

Greater than (`>`)

- **Less than (`<`)**

Greater than or equal to (`>=`)

Less than or equal to (`<=`)

Example:

```groovy
def x = 5 def y = 10
println x == y // Outputs: false println x != y // Outputs: true

println x < y  // Outputs: true
```

4.1.3 Logical Operators

Logical operators allow for the combination of Boolean expressions. Groovy offers three main logical operators:

- **AND (`&&`)**
- **OR (`||`)**
- **NOT (`!`)**

Example:

```groovy
def a = true def b = false
```

```
println a && b  // Outputs: false println a || b  // Outputs:
true println !a       // Outputs: false
```

4.1.4 Bitwise Operators

Bitwise operators perform operations on bits of variables.
Groovy supports the following:

- **AND (`&`)**

- **OR (`|`)**

- **XOR (`^`)**

Complement (`~`)

Left shift (`<<`)

Right shift (`>>`)

Example:

```groovy
def x = 5  // 0101 in binary def y = 3  // 0011 in binary
```

```
println x & y  // Outputs: 1 (0001) println x | y  // Outputs:
7 (0111) println x ^ y  // Outputs: 6 (0110)
```

4.1.5 Assignment Operators

Assignment operators are used to assign values to
variables. Groovy supports several assignment operators,
including:

Simple assignment (`=`)

Add and assign (`+=`)

Subtract and assign (`-=`)

Multiply and assign (`*=`)

Divide and assign (`/=`)

Example:

```groovy

def a = 5
a += 3  // a = a + 3 println a // Outputs: 8
```

4.1.6 Unary Operators

Unary operators operate on a single variable and change its value. In Groovy, you can use:

Unary plus (`+`)

Unary minus (`-`)

Increment (`++`)

Decrement (`--`)

Example:

```groovy defnum = 5 num++
println num // Outputs: 6
```

4.1.7 Conditional (Ternary) Operator

The conditional operator is a shorthand for `if-else` statements that returns one of two values based on a condition. It has the following form:

```groovy
condition ? valueIfTrue : valueIfFalse
```

Example:

```groovy
def age = 18
def canVote = (age >= 18) ? "Yes" : "No" println canVote // Outputs: Yes
```

4.2 Expressions

An expression is a combination of variables, operators, and values that evaluates to a value. Groovy allows you to construct complex expressions using any of the operators detailed above.

4.2.1 Evaluation of Expressions

Expressions in Groovy are evaluated based on the order of operations, following standard mathematical rules (often abbreviated as PEMDAS - Parentheses, Exponents, Multiplication/Division, Addition/Subtraction).

Example:

```groovy
def result = 3 + 5 * 2
println result // Outputs: 13 (5 * 2 is evaluated first)
```

4.2.2 String Interpolation

Groovy supports string interpolation that allows you to embed expressions within strings using the dollar sign `$`.

Example:

```groovy
def name = "Alice"

def greeting = "Hello, $name!"

println greeting // Outputs: Hello, Alice!
```

4.2.3 Using GStrings

GStrings (Groovy Strings) can include expressions, making string manipulation powerful and straightforward.

Example:

```groovy
def price = 20

def discount = 0.1

def message = "With discount, the price is ${price - (price * discount)}" println message // Outputs: With discount, the price is 18.0
```

Understanding operators and expressions is crucial for effective programming in Groovy. The versatility of these operators allows for cleaner and more concise code, while Groovy's flexibility in expressions provides a powerful tool for developers seeking to implement complex logic efficiently. As you advance in your Groovy programming journey, leveraging these operators will enhance your ability to write effective and understandable code. In the next chapter, we will dive deeper into control structures and how they interact with operators and expressions.

Arithmetic and Logical Operators

Groovy, a powerful and dynamic language built on the Java platform, offers a robust set of arithmetic and logical operators that facilitate these tasks seamlessly. In this chapter, we will explore these operators in detail, providing examples and explanations to enhance your understanding and enable you to use them confidently in your Groovy scripts.

1. Arithmetic Operators

Arithmetic operators are fundamental in any programming language, allowing developers to perform basic mathematical operations. In Groovy, the common arithmetic operators are as follows:

1.1 Addition (`+`)

The addition operator is used to sum two or more numeric values. It can also concatenate strings.

```groovy
def sum = 5 + 3

println "The sum of 5 and 3 is: $sum" // Output: The sum of 5 and 3 is: 8

def greeting = "Hello, " + "World!" println greeting // Output: Hello, World!
```

```
```

1.2 Subtraction (`-`)

The subtraction operator calculates the difference between two numeric values.

```groovy
def difference = 10 - 4

println "The difference between 10 and 4 is: $difference" // Output: The difference between 10 and 4 is: 6
```

1.3 Multiplication (`*`)

The multiplication operator is used to multiply two numeric values.

```groovy
def product = 6 * 7

println "The product of 6 and 7 is: $product" // Output: The product of 6 and 7 is: 42
```

1.4 Division (`/`)

The division operator performs division of one numeric value by another.

```groovy
def quotient = 20 / 4

println "The quotient of 20 and 4 is: $quotient" // Output: The quotient of 20 and 4 is: 5.0
```

1.5 Modulus (`%`)

The modulus operator returns the remainder of a division operation.

```groovy
def remainder = 17 % 5

println "The remainder of 17 divided by 5 is: $remainder"
// Output: The remainder of 17 divided by 5 is: 2
```

1.6 Exponentiation (`**`)

Groovy also provides an exponentiation operator to raise a number to a power.

```groovy
def power = 2 ** 3

println "Two raised to the power of three is: $power" // Output: Two raised to the power of three is: 8
```

2. Logical Operators

Logical operators are used to connect and combine Boolean expressions. They are critical for evaluating conditions in control flow statements such as if-else, loops, and more. Groovy provides several logical operators, including:

2.1 Logical AND (`&&`)

The logical AND operator returns `true` if both operands are true.

```groovy
def a = true def b = false
println "a && b is: ${a && b}" // Output: a && b is: false
```

2.2 Logical OR (`||`)

The logical OR operator returns `true` if at least one of the operands is true.

```groovy
println "a || b is: ${a || b}" // Output: a || b is: true
```

2.3 Logical NOT (`!`)

The logical NOT operator inverts the Boolean value of the operand.

```groovy
println "!a is: ${!a}" // Output: !a is: false
```

2.4 Short-Circuit Evaluation

Groovy's logical operators use short-circuit evaluation, meaning that evaluations stop as soon as the result is determined.

```groovy
def x = 5
def y = 10

// In this case, the second condition is never evaluated because the first condition is false if (x > 10 && (y++ > 10)) {
println "This won't execute."
```

```
}
println "y is: $y" // Output: y is: 10
```

3. Combining Arithmetic and Logical Operators

Often, you will find yourself needing to combine arithmetic and logical operators to create more complex expressions. For example, you may want to check whether a number is even and greater than a certain threshold:

```groovy
def number = 14 def threshold = 10

if (number % 2 == 0 && number > threshold) {

println "$number is an even number greater than $threshold"

} else {

println "$number does not meet the criteria."

}
```

In this chapter, we have explored the basic arithmetic and logical operators in Groovy. Understanding these operators is essential for writing effective and efficient scripts because they provide the foundation for performing calculations and evaluating conditions. As you continue to learn and practice Groovy, utilizing these operators will enable you to create more powerful and dynamic applications. In the next chapter, we will delve into control structures, which will further enhance your programming skills by allowing you to dictate the flow of your programs.

Working with Expressions

One of its most powerful features is its ability to handle expressions adeptly. In this chapter, we will explore how to work with expressions in Groovy, providing a deep dive into the types of expressions you can use, their syntax, and practical examples that will help you apply this knowledge.

1. Understanding Expressions

In programming, an expression is a combination of variables, operators, and values that yields a result. In Groovy, expressions can be as simple as numeric literal values or as complex as method calls and closures. They form the fundamental building blocks of Groovy code, enabling developers to create dynamic and flexible applications.

Types of Expressions

Groovy supports several types of expressions:

- **Literal Expressions**: These are fixed values such as numbers, strings, or booleans. For example:

```groovy
def num = 42       // Numeric literal def str = "Hello Groovy" // String literal def truth = true // Boolean literal
```

- **Arithmetic Expressions**: Using arithmetic operators,

64

you can perform calculations.

```groovy
def sum = 5 + 10     // Addition
def product = 4 * 7   // Multiplication
```

- **Comparison Expressions**: These expressions compare two values, resulting in a boolean value.

```groovy
def isEqual = (5 == 5)       // true def isNotEqual = (5 != 4)  // true
```

- **Logical Expressions**: Used to combine boolean values using logical operators like AND (`&&`), OR (`||`), and NOT (`!`).

```groovy
def isTrue = true && false  // false
```

- **String Expressions**: Groovy allows for string interpolation, making it easy to include variables within strings.

```groovy
def name = "Groovy"

def greeting = "Welcome to $name!" // String interpolation
```

2. Expression Syntax

Groovy's syntax is designed to be concise and readable. Here are some key aspects of Groovy expression syntax:

Parentheses

Using parentheses is optional in many cases, but they can help clarify the order of operations or precedence.

```groovy
```groovy def a = 5 def b = 10

def max = (a > b) ? a : b  // Using the ternary operator
```
```

Ternary Operator

The ternary operator is a shorthand for `if-else` statements, simplifying conditional expressions.

```groovy
```groovy

def score = 85

def result = (score >= 60) ? "Passed" : "Failed"
```
```

Safe Navigation Operator

To handle null references gracefully, Groovy provides the safe navigation operator (`?.`). This allows you to safely access properties and methods without throwing a `NullPointerException`.

```groovy
```groovy

def person = null

def name = person?.name  // returns null instead of
```
```

throwing an exception
```

### Elvis Operator

The Elvis operator (`?:`) is a shorthand for the ternary operator that provides a default value when an expression evaluates to null.

```groovy
def input = null

def output = input ?: "Default Value" // output will be "Default Value"
```

3. Closures as Expressions

In Groovy, closures are a powerful feature that allows you to define blocks of code that can be passed around and executed dynamically. They can be used wherever an expression is expected.

```groovy
def add = { num1, num2 -> num1 + num2 } def result = add(5, 10) // result is 15
```

Closure with Higher-Order Functions

Groovy supports passing closures as parameters to other functions, allowing for functional programming paradigms.

```groovy

```groovy
def performOperation(int a, int b, Closure operation) {
    return operation(a, b)
}

def sum = performOperation(5, 10, { x, y -> x + y }) // returns 15
```

4. Practical Examples

Let's put our knowledge of expressions into practice with some examples. ### Example 1: Calculator

Consider creating a simple calculator that handles basic arithmetic operations based on user input.

```groovy
def calculator(int a, int b, String operation) { switch (operation) {

case "+": return a + b

case "-": return a - b

case "*": return a * b

case "/": return a / b

default:

return "Unknown operation"

}

}

def result = calculator(10, 5, "+")

println "Result: $result" // Outputs: Result: 15
```

Example 2: Evaluating Conditions

Utilizing Boolean expressions to evaluate conditions for user permissions.

```groovy
def user = [role: 'admin', isActive: true]

def canEdit = user.role == 'admin' && user.isActive

println "User can edit: $canEdit" // Outputs: User can edit: true
```

Working with expressions in Groovy opens up a world of possibilities for developing robust applications. By mastering the nuances of expressions—from literals and arithmetic to closures—you leverage Groovy's dynamic capabilities effectively. As you continue your journey in Groovy, remember that the strength of the language lies in its ability to express complex logic simply and elegantly. The next chapter will delve into control structures, where we will explore how to control the flow of execution in your Groovy applications.

Chapter 5: Control Structures

Control structures play a vital role in programming by allowing developers to dictate the flow of execution. In this chapter, we will explore the various control structures available in Groovy, including conditional statements, loops, and exception handling.

5.1 Conditional Statements

Conditional statements allow the execution of specific blocks of code based on certain conditions. Groovy provides several ways to perform conditional logic.

5.1.1 If-Else Statement

The `if-else` statement is the most commonly used type of control structure. It executes a block of code if the specified condition is true and optionally executes another block if it is false.

```groovy
def number = 10
if (number > 0) {
println "${number} is positive."
} else {
println "${number} is not positive."
}
```

In the above example, the program checks if `number` is greater than zero and prints the corresponding message.

5.1.2 Else-If Ladder

For multiple conditions, you can use an `if-else if` ladder.

```groovy
def score = 85
if (score >= 90) { println "Grade: A"
} else if (score >= 80) { println "Grade: B"
} else if (score >= 70) { println "Grade: C"
} else {
println "Grade: D"
}
```

This example demonstrates how to categorize a score into different grades based on its value. ### 5.1.3 Switch Statement

Groovy also provides a `switch` statement that can be more readable than multiple `if-else` statements for evaluating a single variable.

```groovy
def day = "Friday"
switch (day) { case "Monday":
println "Start of the week." break
case "Friday":
println "End of the week." break
case "Saturday":
case "Sunday": println "Weekend!" break
```

```groovy
default:
println "Midweek day."
}
```

In this scenario, the program evaluates `day` and executes the matching case block. ## 5.2 Looping Constructs

Looping constructs allow repeated execution of a block of code as long as a condition is true or for a specific number of iterations.

5.2.1 For Loop

The `for` loop in Groovy can iterate over a range or a collection.

```groovy
for (i in 1..5) {
println "Iteration ${i}"
}
```

This loop will print the iteration number from 1 to 5. Groovy's range operator (`..`) is very useful for these types of iterations.

5.2.2 While Loop

A `while` loop continues executing as long as its condition evaluates to `true`.

```groovy
def count = 1
while (count <= 5) {
```

```groovy
println "Count: ${count}" count++
}
```

This loop increments `count` until it reaches 5, printing its value during each iteration. ### 5.2.3 Do-While Loop

The `do-while` loop is similar to the `while` loop, except that it guarantees at least one execution of the loop body.

```groovy
def num = 1 do {
println "Number: ${num}" num++
} while (num <= 5)
```

In this case, the loop prints numbers from 1 to 5, similar to the `while` loop. ## 5.3 Exception Handling

Exception handling in Groovy is fundamentally similar to Java, using `try`, `catch`, `finally`, and `throw` keywords to manage errors gracefully.

5.3.1 Try-Catch

The `try-catch` block enables you to catch exceptions that may occur within the `try` block.

```groovy
try {
def result = 10 / 0
} catch (ArithmeticException e) { println "Cannot divide by zero!"
}
```

In this example, the division by zero causes an `ArithmeticException`, which is caught and handled by the

`catch` block.

5.3.2 Finally Block

The `finally` block will execute regardless of whether an exception was thrown, making it useful for cleanup tasks.

```groovy
def file = null try {

file = new File("example.txt")

// Perform file operations

} catch (FileNotFoundException e) { println "File not found!"

} finally { if (file) {

file.close()

println "File closed."

}

}
```

In this example, whether an exception occurs or not, the `finally` block ensures that the file resource is properly closed.

In this chapter, we explored the various control structures available in Groovy, including conditional statements to execute code based on conditions, loop constructs to repeat actions, and exception handling for managing errors. Understanding these control structures is crucial for developing effective Groovy scripts and applications. As we continue to explore Groovy, these control mechanisms will serve as foundational elements in building more complex logic in your code.

Conditional Statements (if, else, switch)

Conditional statements are a fundamental part of programming and are crucial for controlling the flow of execution within applications. In Groovy, a dynamic programming language that runs on the Java Virtual Machine (JVM), conditional statements provide developers with the means to introduce logic and make decisions based on varying conditions. In this chapter, we will explore the `if`, `else`, and `switch` statements in Groovy, complete with syntax, examples, and best practices.

1. If Statements

The simplest form of a conditional statement in Groovy is the `if` statement. It allows the execution of a block of code based on a specific condition being true.

Syntax

```groovy
if (condition) {
// Code to execute if condition is true
}
```

Example

```groovy
def number = 10
if (number > 5) {
println "The number is greater than 5."
}
```

In this example, the code inside the `if` block executes because the condition `number > 5` evaluates to true.
If-Else Statement

Sometimes, you may want to execute alternative code when the condition is not met. In such cases, the `if- else` structure comes in handy.

Syntax

```groovy
if (condition) {
// Code to execute if condition is true
} else {
// Code to execute if condition is false
}
```

Example

```groovy
```

```groovy
def number = 3
if (number > 5) {
println "The number is greater than 5."
} else {
println "The number is 5 or less."
}
```

In this case, since `number` is not greater than 5, the output will be "The number is 5 or less." ### Else If Statement

For scenarios requiring multiple conditions, the `else if` statement can be utilized to chain conditions together.

Syntax

```groovy
if (condition1) {
// Code for condition 1
} else if (condition2) {
// Code for condition 2
} else {
// Code if none of the above conditions are true
}
```

Example

```groovy
```

```groovy
def number = 0
if (number > 0) {
println "The number is positive."
} else if (number < 0) {
println "The number is negative."
} else {
println "The number is zero."
}
```

This block checks the value of `number` and outputs the appropriate statement based on its value. ## 2. Switch Statements

Switch statements provide a cleaner alternative to multiple `if-else` statements, especially when dealing with a variable that can take on multiple discrete values.

Syntax

```groovy
switch (expression) {
case value1:
// Code to execute if expression equals value1 break
case value2:
// Code to execute if expression equals value2 break
default:
// Code to execute if none of the cases match
```

```
}
```
Example
```groovy
def day = 3
switch (day) { case 1:
println "Monday" break
case 2:
println "Tuesday" break
case 3:
println "Wednesday" break
case 4:
println "Thursday" break
case 5:
println "Friday" break
case 6:
println "Saturday" break
case 7:
println "Sunday" break
default:
println "Invalid day"
}
```

Here, the value of `day` determines which case block

executes, outputting "Wednesday" because `day` has the value 3.

Using Multiple Cases

Switch statements can also handle multiple cases sharing the same block of code. ### Example

```groovy
def grade = 'B'
switch (grade) { case 'A':
case 'B':
case 'C':
println "You passed!" break
case 'D':
case 'F':
println "You failed." break
default:
println "Invalid grade"
}
```

In this example, if `grade` is 'A', 'B', or 'C', the statement "You passed!" is printed. ## 3. Best Practices

Use `else if` Sparingly: While nested conditions can be useful, aim for clarity and readability. Overly complex conditional chains can make code difficult to follow.

Favor `switch` for Multiple Conditions: When you

have multiple distinct values for a single variable, consider using a `switch` statement. It's clearer than a long `if-else` structure.

Consistent Formatting: Maintain consistent indentation and formatting to enhance readability. Properly align braces and know how to position blocks of code.

Utilize Groovy's Flexibility: Groovy allows conditions to be any expression that evaluates to a boolean. This means you can use ranges, collections, and more complex expressions in your conditions.

Avoid Deep Nesting: Deeply nested conditions can lead to hard-to-read code. Refactor your conditionals into methods if they become unwieldy.

Understanding and effectively using conditional statements is essential when programming in Groovy. The

`if`, `else`, and `switch` constructs provide powerful tools for decision-making in code. By mastering these statements and adhering to best practices, you can write clean, maintainable, and efficient Groovy applications that respond intelligently to different inputs and conditions. As you gain more experience with Groovy, you will find these conditional constructs becoming second nature in your programming endeavors.

Looping Constructs (for, while, do-while)

This chapter delves into the looping constructs available in Groovy, specifically focusing on the `for`, `while`, and `do-while` loops. Each type of loop has its appropriate use cases, strengths, and intricacies that make it suited to specific programming scenarios. Understanding these constructs will help you write more efficient and expressive Groovy code.

1. The `for` Loop

The `for` loop is a classic construct that allows you to repeat a block of code a predetermined number of times. It is particularly useful when working with collections or arrays.

Basic Syntax

The typical syntax of a `for` loop in Groovy looks like this:

```groovy
for (initialization; termination; increment) {
// Code to execute
}
```

Initialization: This statement is executed once before the loop starts. It's usually used to define and set up the loop variable.

Termination: This condition is evaluated before each iteration. If it returns `false`, the loop terminates.

Increment: This statement is executed at the end of each iteration. It usually increments or decrements the loop variable.

Example

Here's a simple example of a `for` loop that prints the

first 10 numbers:

```groovy
for (int i = 1; i <= 10; i++) { println "Current number: $i"
}
```

In this example, the loop initializes `i` to 1, checks if it's less than or equal to 10, and increments `i` by 1 after each iteration. It prints the current number on each pass through the loop.

Enhanced `for` Loop

Groovy provides an enhanced version of the `for` loop, often referred to as the "for-each" loop. This is particularly useful for iterating over collections like lists and maps.

```groovy
def numbers = [1, 2, 3, 4, 5] for (number in numbers) {
println "Number: $number"
}
```

Conclusion on `for` Loop

The `for` loop is versatile and ideal for scenarios where you know the range of iteration in advance. Whether you are dealing with primitive types or collections, the `for` construct allows for greater flexibility and readability.

2. The `while` Loop

The `while` loop provides a way to execute a block of code

as long as a specified condition remains true. It is particularly useful when the number of iterations is not known before entering the loop.

Basic Syntax

The syntax for a `while` loop in Groovy is:

```groovy
while (condition) {
// Code to execute
}
```

Example

Here's an example that demonstrates the use of a `while` loop:

```groovy
int count = 1
while (count <= 5) { println "Count is: $count" count++
}
```

In this case, the loop continues until `count` is greater than 5. Inside the loop, we print the current value of `count` and then increment it. ### Conclusion on `while` Loop

The `while` loop is best suited for situations where the number of iterations is not predetermined, allowing the loop to run based on dynamic conditions.

3. The `do-while` Loop

The `do-while` loop is a variation of the `while` loop. The key difference is that the `do-while` loop guarantees that the block of code is executed at least once before evaluating the condition.

Basic Syntax

The syntax for a `do-while` loop is as follows:

```groovy
do {
// Code to execute

} while (condition)
```

Example

Here's an example of a `do-while` loop that guarantees at least one execution:

```groovy
int number = 0 do {
println "Number is: $number" number++
} while (number < 3)
```

In this example, the loop will print the value of `number` until it reaches 3, but it will execute the block at least once before checking the condition.

Choose the `do-while` loop when you want to ensure that the loop body is executed at least once, regardless of the condition's truth value.

Summary of Looping Constructs

In Groovy, the looping constructs (`for`, `while`, and `do-while`) provide flexibility and power to control the flow of your programs.

Use **`for` loops** when you know the number of iterations in advance.

Opt for **`while` loops** when the iterations depend on dynamic conditions.

Choose **`do-while` loops** when you need to guarantee at least one execution of the loop's body.

By mastering these constructs, you can manipulate data more effectively and build rich, interactive applications with Groovy. Remember that thoughtful application of the right looping construct can lead to cleaner and more maintainable code.

Chapter 6: Collections and Arrays

Groovy, being a dynamic language built on the JVM, inherits Java's collection framework while enriching it with additional syntactic sugar. This results in a more fluent and expressive way to handle data structures.

Whether you are managing lists, maps, or sets, Groovy provides a seamless experience that can enhance your coding efficiency and readability.

6.1 Understanding Arrays

An array is a fundamental data structure that represents a fixed-size collection of elements of the same type. In Groovy, arrays can be created using square brackets or the `new` keyword. Despite Groovy's focus on collections, arrays still retain their importance, especially when performance is a consideration.

Creating Arrays

You can create an array in Groovy by using the following syntax:

```groovy
def intArray = [1, 2, 3, 4, 5] // Using square brackets def stringArray = new String[3] // Using 'new' keyword stringArray[0] = "Hello"

stringArray[1] = "Groovy" stringArray[2] = "World"
```

Accessing and Modifying Arrays

Accessing elements in an array is straightforward using the index notation:

```groovy
println(intArray[0]) // Output: 1 intArray[1] = 10
println(intArray[1]) // Output: 10
```

One key limitation of arrays is their fixed size; once defined, the size cannot be altered. If you find yourself needing dynamic resizing, collections such as lists are the better option.

6.2 Collections in Groovy

Groovy provides several collection types, each catering to specific use cases. The most commonly used collections are lists, sets, and maps.

6.2.1 Lists

Lists in Groovy are dynamic arrays that can hold a sequence of elements. They allow duplicate values and maintain insertion order. You can create a list using square brackets:

```groovy
def myList = [1, 2, 3, 4, 5]
```

Adding and Removing Elements

Adding elements is as easy as using the `<<` operator or the `add()` method, while removal can be done with the `remove()` method or the `-=` operator:

```groovy
myList << 6 // Adds 6 to the list myList.add(7) // Adds 7 to the list myList.remove(0) // Removes the first element
```

```groovy
println(myList) // Output: [2, 3, 4, 5, 6, 7]
```

List Iteration

You can iterate over lists in various ways:

```groovy
myList.each { item ->
println(item)
}
```

Or using a simple loop:

```groovy
for (item in myList) { println(item)
}
```

6.2.2 Sets

A set is a collection that contains no duplicate elements. It is useful when you want to prevent duplicate entries. In Groovy, you can create a set using the `as Set` syntax or simply with square brackets:

```groovy
def mySet = [1, 2, 2, 3] as Set // Set will only contain 1, 2, 3
```

Sets can be useful in scenarios where you need to manage unique values, such as in mathematical operations like union and intersection.

6.2.3 Maps

Maps are key-value pairs that allow for easy data retrieval. Maps in Groovy are remarkably flexible, allowing any object type as a key or value:

```groovy
def myMap = [name: "John", age: 30, city: "New York"]
```

You can access and modify map elements using key identifiers:

```groovy
println(myMap['name']) // Output: John

myMap['age'] = 31 // Update age
```

Maps can also be iterated over:

```groovy
myMap.each { key, value -> println("$key: $value")
}
```

6.3 Advanced Collection Operations ### 6.3.1 GDK Methods

The Groovy Development Kit (GDK) extends Java's collections framework with a variety of additional methods that facilitate more complex operations:

find(): Retrieves the first element that matches a

condition.

findAll(): Filters and returns all elements that match a condition.

collect(): Transforms elements in the collection based on a provided function. Example:

```groovy
def numbers = [1, 2, 3, 4, 5]

def evenNumbers = numbers.findAll { it % 2 == 0 } // [2, 4] println(evenNumbers)

def doubled = numbers.collect { it * 2 } // [2, 4, 6, 8, 10] println(doubled)
```

6.3.2 Sorting and Reversing

Collections in Groovy can be sorted using the `sort()` method, either in natural order or a custom order:

```groovy
def unsortedList = [5, 1, 3, 2, 4]

def sortedList = unsortedList.sort() // [1, 2, 3, 4, 5] println(sortedList)

def reversedList = sortedList.reverse() // [5, 4, 3, 2, 1] println(reversedList)
```

In this chapter, we explored the powerful collection and array capabilities of Groovy. Whether you need fixed-size arrays or dynamic collections, Groovy provides an intuitive syntax and flexible methods to effectively manage data. By utilizing lists, sets, and maps, you can write cleaner and more efficient code. Furthermore, the GDK's additional methods enable complex manipulations and data transformations with minimal effort.

As we move forward, keep these data structures in mind as they will serve as the building blocks for more advanced Groovy programming techniques. In the next chapter, we will explore how to handle files and directories in Groovy, further expanding our toolkit for developing robust applications.

Working with Lists and Sets

The primary types of collections offered by Groovy are lists and sets. Each of these collections has unique properties and behaviors, making them suitable for various use cases. Lists maintain the order of elements and allow duplicates, while sets are unordered and prohibit duplicates. In this chapter, we will explore how to work with lists and sets in Groovy, including their creation, manipulation, and important built-in methods.

Understanding Lists

A list in Groovy is an ordered collection that allows duplicate elements. This means that you can have the same item multiple times and retrieve it based on its index. Lists are versatile and are typically used when the order of items is important.

Creating Lists

Creating a list in Groovy is straightforward. You can use the square brackets `[]` to define a list, and you can initialize it with elements:

```groovy
def fruits = ['apple', 'banana', 'orange'] def numbers = [1, 2, 3, 4, 5]
```

You can also create an empty list and add elements later:

```groovy
def emptyList = [] emptyList << 'first' emptyList << 'second'
```

Accessing List Elements

To access elements in a list, simply use the index of the element within square brackets. Remember that indices in Groovy are zero-based:

```groovy
println fruits[0] // Outputs: apple println fruits[1] // Outputs: banana
```

Modifying Lists

Groovy provides several methods to modify lists, including adding, removing, and updating elements. #### Adding Elements

You can add elements to a list using the `<<` operator or the `add()` method:

```groovy
fruits << 'grape'  // Using the addition operator
```

```groovy
fruits.add('pear') // Using the add method
```

Removing Elements

To remove an element, you can use the `remove()` method or the `-=` operator:

```groovy
fruits.remove('banana') // Removes the first occurrence of 'banana' fruits -= 'orange'      // Removes 'orange' using the subtraction operator
```

Updating Elements

Updating elements is done by accessing the element via its index:

```groovy
fruits[0] = 'kiwi' // Changes 'apple' to 'kiwi'
```

Traversing Lists

You can loop through items in a list using various constructs, such as the `each` method or a `for` loop:

```groovy
fruits.each { fruit ->
println fruit
}
// OR
for (fruit in fruits) { println fruit
```

```
}
```

Common List Methods

Groovy lists come with numerous built-in methods that simplify operations. Here are some commonly used methods:

`size()`: Returns the number of elements in the list.

`contains(item)`: Checks if the list contains a specific item.

`sort()`: Sorts the list in natural order.

`reverse()`: Reverses the order of items in the list. ## Understanding Sets

A set in Groovy is an unordered collection of unique elements. The primary use case for sets is when you want to ensure that all items are distinct, such as user IDs or unique tags.

Creating Sets

Creating a set in Groovy can be accomplished using the `Set` interface or simply by using curly braces `{}`. Here's how you can do it:

```groovy
def uniqueFruits = ['apple', 'banana', 'orange'] as Set

def numbersSet = [1, 2, 3, 4, 4, 5] as Set   // Duplicates are automatically removed.
```

Adding and Removing Elements

Just like lists, sets support adding and removing elements using similar methods:

```groovy
uniqueFruits << 'grape'    // Add 'grape'
uniqueFruits.add('kiwi') // Add another fruit

uniqueFruits.remove('banana') // Remove 'banana'

uniqueFruits -= 'apple'    // Remove 'apple' using the subtraction operator
```

Traversing Sets

You can iterate through a set using the same methods as with lists:

```groovy
uniqueFruits.each { fruit ->
println fruit
}
// OR
for (fruit in uniqueFruits) { println fruit
}
```

Common Set Methods

Sets also come with useful methods that facilitate common operations:

`size()`: Returns the number of elements in the set.

`contains(item)`: Checks if the set contains a specific item.

`intersect(otherSet)`: Returns elements that are common to both sets.

`subtract(otherSet)`: Returns elements that are in the calling set but not in the specified set.

Working with lists and sets in Groovy provides a flexible and dynamic way to handle collections of data. Lists are perfect for situations where order is important and duplicates are acceptable, while sets are ideal for maintaining uniqueness amongst elements. Understanding these collections, along with their associated methods, is essential for writing effective Groovy code. By mastering lists and sets, you will be better equipped to handle complex data structures and build robust applications.

As you continue to explore Groovy, you will find that collections play an essential role in various programming tasks, making them a key concept in your development toolkit.

Using Maps and Arrays

One of the language's strengths is its support for complex data structures, notably maps and arrays. These structures allow developers to manage collections of data effectively, making it easier to write readable and maintainable code. In this chapter, we will explore how to use maps and arrays in Groovy, including their creation, manipulation, and when to choose one over the other.

Understanding Arrays in Groovy

An array is a fixed-size collection of elements of the same type. In Groovy, you can create arrays with a simple syntax. Below are some of the common operations involving arrays:

Creating Arrays

To create an array in Groovy, you can use the following syntax:

```groovy
def fruits = ["Apple", "Banana", "Cherry"]
```

This creates an array named `fruits` containing three string elements. Note that Groovy supports dynamic typing, so you can even mix types in an array, although it is recommended to maintain a consistent type for clarity.

Accessing Elements

You can access elements of an array using their index, which starts from 0. Here's an example:

```groovy
println(fruits[0]) // Output: Apple
```

Modifying Elements

You can change the value of an array element by directly assigning a new value:

```groovy
fruits[1] = "Blueberry"
println(fruits) // Output: [Apple, Blueberry, Cherry]
```

```

```

Array Length

To get the length of an array, use the `length` property:

```groovy
println(fruits.length) // Output: 3
```

Iterating Through Arrays

Groovy simplifies the process of iterating through arrays:

```groovy
fruits.each { fruit ->
println(fruit)
}
```

You can also use traditional for-loops if you prefer:

```groovy
for (int i = 0; i < fruits.length; i++) { println(fruits[i])
}
```

Understanding Maps in Groovy

Maps are a more flexible and dynamic data structure compared to arrays. A map is a collection of key-value pairs, allowing you to retrieve values based on unique keys.

Creating Maps

To create a map in Groovy, you can use the following syntax:

```groovy
def person = [name: "John Doe", age: 30, occupation: "Developer"]
```

This creates a map named `person` with three key-value pairs. The keys in Groovy maps can be any type, including strings and integers.

Accessing Values

You can retrieve values from a map using the key:

```groovy
println(person["name"]) // Output: John Doe
```

You can also access values using the dot notation (for keys that are valid identifiers):

```groovy
println(person.name) // Output: John Doe
```

Modifying Values

Changing the value associated with a key is straightforward:

```groovy
person["age"] = 31
```

println(person) // Output: [name:John Doe, age:31, occupation:Developer]

```
```

Adding and Removing Entries

To add a new key-value pair:
```groovy
person["email"] = "johndoe@example.com"
```

To remove an entry:
```groovy
person.remove("occupation")
println(person)  // Output: [name:John Doe, age:31, email:johndoe@example.com]
```

Iterating Through Maps

You can iterate through maps using the `each` method to access both keys and values:

```groovy
person.each { key, value -> println("$key: $value")
}
```

When to Use Arrays vs. Maps

Choosing between arrays and maps depends on the specific requirements of your application:

Arrays are suitable for ordered collections where you need to access elements by their index. They are ideal when the number of elements is known in advance and

101

there is a consistent type across all elements.

Maps provide more flexibility for storing data when you need to access values by meaningful keys. They are useful for representing complex data structures, such as JSON-like objects, where the relationship between keys and values is important.

By understanding their strengths and functionalities, you can write more efficient and organized code. Whether you're managing lists of items or representing complex data structures, Groovy's collections are immensely powerful tools that can significantly enhance your programming experience. As you continue developing with Groovy, practice using these data structures to become more proficient in handling data within your applications.

Chapter 7: Functions and Closures

In Groovy, functions are treated as first-class citizens, meaning you can assign them to variables, pass them as arguments, and return them from other functions. This flexibility allows for a functional programming style that can lead to more concise and expressive code.

Defining Functions

In Groovy, functions are defined using the `def` keyword followed by the function name and parentheses. Here's a simple example:

```groovy
def greet(String name) { return "Hello, ${name}!"
}
println(greet("Alice"))
```

In this example, we define a function named `greet` that takes a single parameter, `name`, and returns a greeting string. Notice how we use string interpolation to include the value of `name` in the output.

Function Overloading

Groovy supports method overloading, allowing you to define multiple functions with the same name but different parameter types or counts. Here's how it works:

```groovy
def greet(String name) { return "Hello, ${name}!"
}
```

```groovy
def greet(String firstName, String lastName) { return "Hello, ${firstName} ${lastName}!"
}

println(greet("Alice"))       // Calls the first greet function
println(greet("Alice", "Smith")) // Calls the second greet function
```

The correct function is chosen based on the number and types of arguments passed, showcasing the flexibility of Groovy's type system.

Closures: A Powerful Feature

Closures in Groovy can be thought of as anonymous functions that can capture the surrounding context. They provide a way to encapsulate behavior and can be passed around as objects. Closures are a powerful feature that enables functional programming techniques.

Creating Closures

You can create a closure using curly braces `{}`. Here's an example of a simple closure:

```groovy
def square = { int number -> number * number }

println(square(5)) // Outputs: 25
```

In this case, `square` is a closure that takes a single integer parameter and returns that number squared. ### Capturing Context with Closures

One of the most powerful aspects of closures is their

104

ability to capture variables from the surrounding scope. This can be illustrated in the following example:

```groovy
def multiplier = 3

def multiply = { int number -> number * multiplier }

println(multiply(5)) // Outputs: 15
```

In this case, the `multiply` closure captures the `multiplier` variable from its surrounding scope, demonstrating how closures maintain a reference to their context.

Closures as First-Class Objects

Closures are first-class objects in Groovy, meaning you can pass them as arguments to other methods or return them from methods. Here's an example of a method that accepts a closure as an argument:

```groovy
def applyOperation(int number, Closure operation) {
return operation(number)
}

def result = applyOperation(5, { it * it * it }) // Calculates the cube of 5 println(result) // Outputs: 125
```

In this case, we define a method `applyOperation` that takes an integer and a closure. The closure is invoked within the method, and we pass it an anonymous closure that calculates the cube of the number.

Higher-Order Functions

Higher-order functions are functions that can take other functions or closures as parameters or return them as results. Groovy makes it easy to work with higher-order functions, allowing developers to leverage powerful functional programming paradigms.

Using Built-in Collection Methods with Closures

Groovy collections come equipped with numerous methods that can leverage closures. For example, the

`collect` method can transform a collection by applying a closure to each element:

```groovy
def numbers = [1, 2, 3, 4, 5]


def squares = numbers.collect { it * it } println(squares)
// Outputs: [1, 4, 9, 16, 25]
```

Moreover, the `find` method can be used to filter collections based on a condition defined in a closure:

```groovy
def evens = numbers.findAll { it % 2 == 0 } println(evens)
// Outputs: [2, 4]
```

Closures and Recursion

Closures can be used for recursive operations. In Groovy, you can assign a closure to a variable and call it recursively. Here's a simple example demonstrating this:

```groovy
def factorial = { int n ->
n == 0 ? 1 : n * factorial(n - 1)
}
println(factorial(5)) // Outputs: 120
```

In this example, the `factorial` closure calculates the factorial of a number using recursion. It checks if `n` is zero, returning `1`, or else it multiplies `n` by a call to itself with `(n - 1)`.

Functions and closures are core components of Groovy that provide versatility in programming. The ability to treat functions as first-class objects, utilize closures to capture context, and implement higher-order functions enhances the expressiveness of the language. As you continue your journey in Groovy programming, mastering functions and closures will empower you to write code that is not only effective but also elegant and concise. In the following chapter, we will explore how to integrate Groovy with Java and leverage both languages to their fullest potential.

Defining and Calling Functions

Among its rich features are the ability to define and call functions, which are essential for structuring code and improving reusability. This chapter delves into how to define and call functions in Groovy, along with best practices and various nuances that make Groovy's function handling unique.

Understanding Functions

In Groovy, functions are defined using the `def` keyword, followed by the function name and parentheses that may contain parameters. Functions enable you to group reusable blocks of code, which can be invoked whenever required.

Basic Function Definition

Let's start with the simplest form of a function:

```groovy
def greet() {
println "Hello, World!"
}
```

In the example above, we defined a function called `greet` that prints out a simple greeting. To call this function, simply use its name followed by parentheses:

```groovy
greet()
```

Upon execution, this will output:

```
Hello, World!
```

Function Parameters

Functions can have parameters, which allow you to customize their behavior. For instance, you can modify the `greet` function to accept a name:

```groovy
def greet(String name) { println "Hello, ${name}!"
}
```

Now, you can call the function with an argument:

```groovy greet("Alice")
```

This will output:

```
Hello, Alice!
```

Default Parameter Values

Groovy also supports default parameter values, allowing you to call the function without specifying all arguments:

```groovy
def greet(String name = "World") { println "Hello, ${name}!"
```

```
}
```

greet()// Outputs: Hello, World! greet("Bob") // Outputs: Hello, Bob!

```
```

Returning Values from Functions

Functions in Groovy can return values. The last evaluated expression in the function body is returned by default, but you can also use the `return` keyword explicitly.

Here's how you might create a function that adds two numbers:

```groovy
def add(int a, int b) { return a + b
}
int sum = add(5, 3)
println "Sum: ${sum}" // Outputs: Sum: 8
```

In this example, the `add` function takes two integer parameters and returns their sum. ## Function Overloading

Groovy supports function overloading, which allows you to define multiple functions with the same name but different parameter types or counts. Here's an example:

```groovy
def multiply(int a, int b) { return a * b
}
def multiply(double a, double b) { return a * b
```

110

```
}
println multiply(2, 3)        // Outputs: 6
println multiply(2.5, 3.5)    // Outputs: 8.75
```

The Groovy runtime selects the appropriate function based on the arguments passed during the function call.
Closures as Functions

In Groovy, closures are a more powerful and flexible way to define functions. A closure is essentially a block of code that can take parameters and can be executed at a later time. Here's a simple example:

```groovy
def square = { int number -> return number * number
}
println square(4) // Outputs: 16
```

Closures can be passed as parameters to functions, stored in variables, and returned from other closures, providing a functional programming style that enhances Groovy's capabilities.

In this chapter, we explored the basics of defining and calling functions in Groovy. We covered parameter passing, default values, return values, function overloading, and the introduction of closures as an alternative to traditional functions. Mastering these concepts is vital for harnessing the full power of Groovy and writing clean, reusable, and efficient code.

Understanding and Using Closures

A closure in Groovy is essentially a block of code that can be assigned to a variable, passed as an argument, or returned from a method. This chapter explores what closures are, how they work, and practical examples of using closures to simplify your code.

What is a Closure?

In simple terms, a closure is an anonymous block of code that can capture variables from its surrounding context. This means that it can access the state of its enclosing environment even after that environment has completed execution. The syntax for defining a closure is concise and intuitive:

```groovy
def myClosure = { param1, param2 ->

// Closure body

println "Hello, $param1 and $param2!"

}
```

In this example, `myClosure` is a closure that takes two parameters and prints a greeting. ## Characteristics of Closures

1. First-Class Citizens

Closures in Groovy are first-class citizens, which means they can be treated like any other object. You can assign them to variables, pass them as arguments to other methods, and return them from methods. This functionality opens up a world of possibilities for functional programming.

2. Capturing Variables

One of the most powerful aspects of closures is their ability to capture variables from their surrounding context. For instance, when you define a closure inside a method, it can access variables from that method's scope:

```groovy
def foo() {

def greeting = "Hello"

def greetClosure = { name -> println "$greeting, $name!"

}

greetClosure("Groovy") // Outputs: Hello, Groovy!

}
foo()
```

Here, `greeting` is captured by `greetClosure`. Even after `foo()` has finished executing, the closure retains access to `greeting`.

3. Higher-Order Functions

Closures can be used as higher-order functions, which are functions that can take other functions as parameters or return them. This allows you to create highly reusable and modular code. For example:

```groovy
def applyClosure(closure, value) { return closure(value)
```

113

```
}
```

```groovy
def multiplyByTwo = { num -> num * 2 }

def result = applyClosure(multiplyByTwo, 5) println result
// Outputs: 10
```

In this example, `applyClosure` takes a closure and a value, applying the closure to the value and returning the result.

Using Closures in Collections

Groovy's collection framework heavily leverages closures, providing several methods that accept closures for streamlined data manipulation. Here are some commonly used methods:

`each()`

The `each()` method iterates over a collection, allowing you to perform an action on each element:

```groovy
def numbers = [1, 2, 3, 4, 5] numbers.each { number ->

println number * number // Prints each number squared

}
```

`find()`

The `find()` method returns the first element that matches a given condition defined in a closure:

```groovy
def result = numbers.find { it > 3 } println result //
```

Outputs: 4
```

### `collect()`

The `collect()` method transforms each element in a collection based on a closure:

```groovy
def doubled = numbers.collect { it * 2 } println doubled // Outputs: [2, 4, 6, 8, 10]
```

`filter()`

While not a built-in method in the same sense as `find()`, you can use `findAll()` to retrieve all elements matching a condition:

```groovy
def evenNumbers = numbers.findAll { it % 2 == 0 } println evenNumbers // Outputs: [2, 4]
```

Practical Examples of Closures ### 1. Sorting a List

You can use closures to customize the sorting behavior with the `sort()` method:

```groovy
def names = ["John", "Jane", "Jack", "Jill"] names.sort { a, b -> a.length() <=> b.length() } println names // Outputs: [John, Jane, Jack, Jill]
```

2. Building a Simple Event Listener

115
```

Closures are incredibly useful for building event-driven applications:

```groovy
class Button {
def onClickClosure
void click() {
if (onClickClosure) { onClickClosure()
}
}
}
def button = new Button()
button.onClickClosure = { println "Button was clicked!" }
button.click() // Outputs: Button was clicked!
```

3. Configuring DSL (Domain-Specific Languages)

Closures can also be used to create intuitive DSLs, allowing developers to specify configurations in a readable manner:

```groovy
def configureDatabase(closure) { def config = [:]
closure.delegate = config closure()
return config
}
def dbConfig = configureDatabase {
url = 'jdbc:mysql://localhost:3306/mydb' user = 'root'
password = 'secret'
```

116

```
}
println          dbConfig          //          Outputs:
[url:jdbc:mysql://localhost:3306/mydb,          user:root,
password:secret]
```
```

Closures significantly enhance the flexibility and power of
Groovy as a programming language. They allow for
concise code, simplify operations on collections, facilitate
event-driven designs, and enable the creation of DSLs. As
you become more comfortable with closures, you'll find
that they become an essential tool in your Groovy toolkit,
paving the way for cleaner, more maintainable, and
expressive programming patterns. Embrace closures,
explore their capabilities, and witness how they can
transform your coding experience in Groovy.
```

Chapter 8: Object-Oriented Programming in Groovy

In this chapter, we will explore the principles of OOP in Groovy, including classes, objects, inheritance, polymorphism, and encapsulation. We will also discuss how Groovy enhances traditional OOP concepts with its dynamic typing, closures, and other syntactic conveniences.

8.1 Understanding Classes and Objects

In Groovy, everything revolves around classes and objects. A class is a blueprint for creating objects (instances), and an object is an instance of a class that can hold state (data) and behavior (methods).

8.1.1 Defining a Class

Defining a class in Groovy is straightforward. Here's a simple example of a `Person` class:

```groovy
class Person {

String name int age

// Constructor
Person(String name, int age) { this.name = name

this.age = age

}

// Method to display person details String displayInfo() {

return "Name: ${name}, Age: ${age}"

}

}
```

```
```

8.1.2 Creating Objects

Once a class is defined, you can create an object of that class using the `new` keyword:

```groovy
def person1 = new Person("Alice", 30)
println(person1.displayInfo()) // Outputs: Name: Alice, Age: 30
```

8.2 Inheritance

Inheritance is one of the core principles of OOP, allowing a new class to inherit properties and methods from an existing class. This promotes code reuse and establishes a hierarchical relationship between classes.

8.2.1 Defining a Subclass

Groovy uses the `extends` keyword to create a subclass. For instance, if we want to create a `Student` class that inherits from `Person`, we can do so as follows:

```groovy
class Student extends Person { String major
```

Student(String name, int age, String major) { super(name, age) // Call to the parent constructor this.major = major

}

@Override

String displayInfo() {

return "${super.displayInfo()}, Major: ${major}"

```
}
}
```

8.2.2 Using Inherited Methods

You can create an instance of the `Student` class and observe the inherited methods:

```groovy
def student1 = new Student("Bob", 21, "Computer Science") println(student1.displayInfo()) // Outputs: Name: Bob, Age: 21, Major: Computer Science
```

8.3 Polymorphism

Polymorphism allows methods to do different things based on the object's runtime type. In Groovy, this is often achieved through method overriding.

```groovy
def displayPersonInfo(Person person) { println(person.displayInfo())
}
displayPersonInfo(person1) // Outputs: Name: Alice, Age: 30 displayPersonInfo(student1) // Outputs: Name: Bob, Age: 21, Major: Computer Science
```

In the above code, the method `displayPersonInfo` can accept both `Person` and `Student` objects, demonstrating polymorphic behavior.

8.4 Encapsulation

Encapsulation is about bundling the data (attributes) and methods (behavior) together and restricting access to some of the object's components. In Groovy, you can define properties with varying access levels, leveraging public, private, and protected keywords.

8.4.1 Property Access Modifiers

Here's how you can restrict access to properties:

```groovy
class BankAccount { private double balance

BankAccount(double initialDeposit) { this.balance = initialDeposit

}

double getBalance() { return balance

}

void deposit(double amount) { balance += amount

}

void withdraw(double amount) { if (amount <= balance) {

balance -= amount

} else {

println("Insufficient funds.")

}

}

}
```

```
```

In this example, the `balance` property cannot be accessed directly from outside the class, ensuring that it's only modified through the provided methods.

8.5 Dynamic Typing and Closures

One of Groovy's most attractive features is its dynamic typing, allowing you to write flexible and adaptable code. Additionally, Groovy's support for closures provides a powerful way to handle behavior.

Closures can be used as parameters, and they can capture the context in which they're defined, making them incredibly versatile.

```groovy
def performOperation(int a, int b, Closure operation) {
operation(a, b)

}

performOperation(5, 3, { x, y -> println("Sum: ${x + y}") }) // Outputs: Sum: 8 performOperation(5, 3, { x, y -> println("Difference: ${x - y}") }) // Outputs: Difference: 2
```

In this chapter, we explored the essential features of object-oriented programming in Groovy, including the creation of classes and objects, inheritance, polymorphism, and encapsulation. We also looked at some of Groovy's unique features, like dynamic typing and closures, which enhance the traditional OOP paradigm. With these tools at your disposal, you can create clean, modular, and maintainable code, paving the way for powerful Groovy applications.

Classes and Objects

Groovy, being a dynamic language that runs on the Java platform, embraces these concepts while offering flexibility and ease of use. This chapter will delve into the intricacies of classes and objects in Groovy, demonstrating how to create and utilize them to enhance code organization and efficiency.

Understanding Classes

A class in Groovy serves as a blueprint for creating objects. It encapsulates properties (attributes) and methods (behaviors) that define the characteristics and functionalities of the objects instantiated from it. The basic syntax for defining a class in Groovy is straightforward, allowing developers to focus on functionality rather than boilerplate code.

Here is a simple example of a class definition in Groovy:

```groovy
class Car {
String make String model int year

void displayDetails() {
println "Car Make: $make, Model: $model, Year: $year"
}
}
```

In this example, we've defined a `Car` class with three properties: `make`, `model`, and `year`. There's also a method called `displayDetails()` that outputs the car's details to the console. Properties in Groovy can be defined without explicit getter and setter methods, as Groovy

123

automatically generates them.

Creating Objects

An object is an instance of a class. In Groovy, creating an object is as simple as calling the class constructor using the `new` keyword. Here's how you can create objects of the `Car` class we defined earlier:

```groovy
Car myCar = new Car(make: 'Toyota', model: 'Camry', year: 2020) myCar.displayDetails()
```

In this code, we instantiate the `Car` class by passing the required parameters using named arguments (a feature that Groovy supports), which enhances readability and reduces the chances of errors.

Properties and Methods #### Properties

Properties in Groovy classes are typically declared at the class level. You can access and modify these properties directly. Groovy offers a syntactical sugar for property access, making it natural and intuitive:

```groovy
myCar.year = 2021 // Modify the year property println myCar.year // Accessing the year property
```

Groovy also supports other data types, enabling you to create more complex classes based on real-world requirements.

Methods

Methods are functions defined in a class that describe its behavior. In Groovy, methods can have optional parameters, default values, and even variable argument lists. Here's an example that demonstrates various functionalities:

```groovy
class Car {

String make String model int year

void drive(int distance) {

println "Driving $distance miles..."

}

void displayDetails(String prefix = "Details:") {

println "$prefix Make: $make, Model: $model, Year: $year"

}

}

Car myCar = new Car(make: 'Honda', model: 'Civic', year: 2019) myCar.drive(150)

myCar.displayDetails()
```

Constructors

In Groovy, constructors initialize objects when they are created. You can define a custom constructor to set initial property values. Here's an example that extends the previous `Car` class with a constructor:

```groovy
class Car {

String make String model int year
```

```groovy
Car(String make, String model, int year) { this.make = make

this.model = model this.year = year
}
void displayDetails() {

println "Car Make: $make, Model: $model, Year: $year"

}
}
Car myCar = new Car('Ford', 'Mustang', 2021)
myCar.displayDetails()
```

Inheritance

Inheritance is a powerful feature in OOP that allows a class to derive properties and behaviors from another class. In Groovy, creating a subclass is straightforward:

```groovy
class ElectricCar extends Car { int batteryCapacity

ElectricCar(String make, String model, int year, int batteryCapacity) { super(make, model, year) // Call the superclass constructor this.batteryCapacity = batteryCapacity

}
void displayDetails() { super.displayDetails()

println "Battery Capacity: $batteryCapacity kWh"

}
```

126

```
}
```

ElectricCar myElectricCar = new ElectricCar('Tesla', 'Model 3', 2022, 75) myElectricCar.displayDetails()
```
` ` `
```

In this example, `ElectricCar` inherits properties from the `Car` class and adds its own property,

`batteryCapacity`. The `super` keyword allows us to invoke the parent class constructor.

Classes and objects are at the heart of Groovy programming, mirroring the practicalities and principles of object-oriented design. By leveraging these concepts, developers can create scalable, maintainable, and reusable code that aligns well with Groovy's expressive syntax and features. As you continue to explore Groovy, keep experimenting with classes and objects to deepen your understanding and harness the full potential of this versatile language.

Inheritance and Polymorphism

In this chapter, we'll explore how Groovy implements these concepts, how they differ from traditional Java syntax, and their practical implications for developers.

Understanding Inheritance ### What is Inheritance?

Inheritance is the mechanism by which one class (the child or subclass) inherits properties and behaviors (i.e., methods) from another class (the parent or superclass). This provides a way to create a new class based on an existing class, allowing for reuse of code and the creation of hierarchical relationships between classes.

Inheritance in Groovy

In Groovy, class inheritance works similarly to Java, but with some syntactic sugar that makes it more concise. A class can extend another class using the `extends` keyword. Here's a basic example:

```groovy
class Animal {
String name
void speak() {
println("The animal makes a sound.")
}
}
class Dog extends Animal { void speak() {
println("${name} barks!")
}
}
```

In this example, `Dog` inherits properties from `Animal`, including the `name` field. It also overrides the

`speak` method to provide a specific implementation for dogs. This is a critical point in OOP as it allows subclasses to customize behaviors while retaining the structure and attributes of the parent class.

Constructor Inheritance

Constructors in Groovy can also be inherited, but it's

essential to remember that if you define a constructor in a subclass, the parent class constructor must be explicitly called if it exists.

```groovy
class Cat extends Animal { Cat(String name) {

super(name) // calling the superclass constructor

}

void speak() { println("${name} meows!")

}

}

def kitty = new Cat("Whiskers") kitty.speak() // Outputs: Whiskers meows!
```

Polymorphism in Groovy ### What is Polymorphism?

Polymorphism allows methods to do different things based on the object that it is acting upon, essentially enabling a single entity to take many forms. Polymorphism is often evidenced through method overriding and method overloading.

Method Overriding

As demonstrated earlier, method overriding is a core aspect of polymorphism in Groovy. Both the superclass and subclass can define a method with the same name, but the implementation in the subclass will be invoked when the method is called on an instance of the subclass.

```groovy
```

129

```groovy
def myDog = new Dog(name: "Buddy") myDog.speak() // Outputs: Buddy barks!
def myCat = new Cat(name: "Mittens") myCat.speak() // Outputs: Mittens meows!
```

Here, `speak` is a polymorphic method that resolves at runtime, resulting in different outputs based on the object type.

Method Overloading

Method overloading refers to the ability to define multiple methods with the same name but different parameters. Groovy supports method overloading, and it can be as simple as changing the type or number of parameters.

```groovy
class MathOperations { int add(int a, int b) {
return a + b
}
double add(double a, double b) { return a + b
}
int add(int a, int b, int c) { return a + b + c
}
}
def math = new MathOperations() println(math.add(2, 3))     // Outputs: 5
println(math.add(2.5, 3.1))// Outputs: 5.6
println(math.add(1, 2, 3))  // Outputs: 6
```
130

```
```

In this example, the `add` method is overloaded with different signatures, showcasing polymorphism through the method name alone across different contexts.

Interfaces and Abstract Classes

Inheritance and polymorphism can also be implemented using interfaces and abstract classes. Interfaces define a contract that implementing classes must fulfill, while abstract classes can provide some base functionality while mandating that certain methods be implemented by subclasses.

Interfaces

Interfaces in Groovy allow for multiple inheritance, enabling a class to implement more than one interface.

```groovy
interface AnimalSounds { void sound()
}
class Duck implements AnimalSounds { void sound() {
println("Quack!")
}
}
class Cow implements AnimalSounds { void sound() {
println("Moo!")
}
}
```

```
` ` `
```

Abstract Classes

Abstract classes provide a mechanism to define a base class that cannot be instantiated on its own but can still provide default implementations to its subclasses.

```groovy
abstract class Shape { abstract double area()

void displayArea() { println("Area: ${area()}")
}
}
class Circle extends Shape { double radius
Circle(double radius) { this.radius = radius
}
@Override double area() {
return Math.PI * radius * radius
}
}
def circle = new Circle(5)
circle.displayArea() // Outputs: Area: 78.53981633974483
```

By leveraging these principles, developers can create robust applications with cleaner designs. Groovy's syntax allows for a more readable and idiomatic approach to these concepts while maintaining compatibility with

Java's OOP principles. Understanding these concepts deeply will enhance your Groovy programming capabilities, allowing you to build more complex and well-structured applications efficiently.

Chapter 9: Exception Handling

Exception handling serves as a mechanism to gracefully catch and manage these errors, ensuring the robustness and reliability of your applications. Groovy, a versatile language built on the Java platform, not only inherits Java's exception handling capabilities but also adds its own syntactical sugar that simplifies error management. In this chapter, we will explore exception handling in Groovy, covering the fundamental concepts, best practices, and some unique Groovy features that enhance error management.

Understanding Exceptions

An exception is an event that disrupts the normal flow of a program's execution. In Java, exceptions are categorized primarily into two types: checked exceptions and unchecked exceptions. Checked exceptions must be either caught or declared in the method signature, while unchecked exceptions do not have such requirements.

Common Exception Types in Groovy

Runtime Exceptions: These are the unchecked exceptions that can occur during the execution of the program, such as NullPointerException, ArrayIndexOutOfBoundsException, and ClassCastException.

Checked Exceptions: These exceptions, such as IOException or SQLException, must be handled explicitly.

Custom Exceptions: Groovy allows developers to create their own exception classes to handle specific error scenarios in a more meaningful way.

Basic Exception Handling ### Try-Catch Block

The most common way to handle exceptions in Groovy is by using a try-catch block. The code that might throw an exception is placed inside the `try` block, while the response to the exception is defined in the

`catch` block.

```groovy
try {
```

// Code that may throw an exception def file = new File('nonexistent.txt') def reader = new FileReader(file)

```groovy
} catch (FileNotFoundException e) { println "File not found: ${e.message}"
```

```groovy
} catch (IOException e) {
```

println "An I/O error occurred: ${e.message}"

```groovy
} finally {
```

println "This block is always executed."

```groovy
}
```
```

### Multiple Catch Blocks

You can catch multiple exceptions in a single try-catch structure by using separate catch blocks. This approach allows you to handle different exceptions in specific ways.

```groovy
try {
```

// Code that may throw exceptions

```groovy
} catch (FileNotFoundException e) {
```

println "Caught a FileNotFoundException: ${e.message}"
```

```
} catch (IOException e) {
println "Caught an IOException: ${e.message}"
} catch (Exception e) {
println "Caught a general exception: ${e.message}"
}
```

The `finally` Block

The `finally` block is optional but very useful. It allows developes to execute a block of code regardless of whether an exception was thrown or not. This is particularly beneficial for closing resources like files or database connections.

```groovy
FileReader reader = null try {
reader = new FileReader('file.txt')
// Read from the file
} catch (FileNotFoundException e) { println "File not found!"
} finally {
if (reader) { reader.close()
println "File reader closed."
}
}
```

Rethrowing Exceptions

Sometimes, you may wish to catch an exception and, after performing some processing, rethrow it for further handling at a higher level in the call stack.

```groovy
try {
// Some code that might throw an exception
} catch (Exception e) {

println "Handling exception: ${e.message}" throw e // Rethrowing the exception

}
```

Custom Exception Classes

Creating custom exceptions can enhance readability and maintainability of your code. This allows you to define a clearly understood error type for specific circumstances.

```groovy
class CustomException extends Exception { CustomException(String message) {

super(message)

}

}

try {

throw new CustomException("This is a custom error.")

} catch (CustomException e) {

println "Caught custom exception: ${e.message}"

}
```

` ` `

Exception Handling Best Practices

Catch Specific Exceptions: Always catch specific exceptions rather than a general `Exception`. This enhances clarity and reduces the risk of unintentionally catching unrelated errors.

Avoid Silent Failures: Do not catch an exception and do nothing. At the very least, log the error. This will assist in debugging and maintaining application reliability.

Clean Up Resources: Use `finally` blocks or try-with-resources (for Java interop) to ensure that resources are always freed, avoiding memory leaks or deadlocks.

Meaningful Error Messages: Provide clear and meaningful error messages to help future developers understand what went wrong.

Use Custom Exceptions Thoughtfully: Custom exceptions can greatly assist in making error handling more manageable, but overusing them can clutter your code. Use them judiciously.

Exception handling is an essential aspect of Groovy programming that contributes significantly to the stability and reliability of applications. Understanding how to use try-catch blocks, deal with various types of exceptions, create custom exceptions, and follow best practices will empower developers to write cleaner and more effective code. In the next chapter, we will explore additional Groovy features such as closures, providing you with more advanced techniques to enhance your programming skills.

Understanding Exceptions

In Groovy, a dynamic programming language built on the Java platform, exception handling is similar to that in Java, but with some unique features that make it more flexible and expressive. This chapter will provide a comprehensive understanding of how exceptions work in Groovy, including how to throw, catch, and handle them, as well as best practices for managing exceptions effectively.

What are Exceptions?

An exception is an event that disrupts the normal flow of a program's execution. In Groovy, just like in Java, exceptions can arise due to various reasons: file handling errors, network connectivity issues, invalid user input, or logical errors in the code. When an exception occurs, Groovy creates an instance of the exception class, which inherits from the `Throwable` class. This instance can then be thrown and caught using appropriate exception handling mechanisms.

Types of Exceptions

Groovy recognizes two main categories of exceptions:

Checked Exceptions: These are exceptions that must be either caught or declared in the method signature. For example, `IOException` or `SQLException` are checked exceptions that require handling.

Unchecked Exceptions: These include `RuntimeException` and its subclasses, such as `NullPointerException` or `ArrayIndexOutOfBoundsException`. Unchecked

139

exceptions do not need to be declared or caught, as they typically indicate programming errors that should be fixed rather than handled.

Throwing Exceptions

In Groovy, we can throw exceptions using the `throw` keyword. When throwing an exception, it is essential to provide an instance of the exception class.

Example: Throwing an Exception

```groovy
def divide(a, b) { if (b == 0) {

throw new IllegalArgumentException("Denominator cannot be zero")

}

return a / b

}
```

In this example, the `divide` method throws an `IllegalArgumentException` if the denominator is zero. This proactive error handling helps prevent runtime issues later in the program.

Catching Exceptions

To handle exceptions in Groovy, we use the `try-catch` block. Code that might throw an exception is placed in the `try` block, and the handling code is placed in the `catch` block. Groovy's syntax allows for multiple

`catch` clauses to handle different types of exceptions.

Example: Catching Exceptions

```groovy
def safeDivide(a, b) { try {

return divide(a, b)

} catch (IllegalArgumentException e) { println "Error: ${e.message}"

} catch (Exception e) {

println "An unexpected error occurred: ${e.message}"

}

}
```

In this implementation, the `safeDivide` method attempts to call the `divide` method. If an

`IllegalArgumentException` is thrown, it is caught and handled gracefully, preventing the program from crashing.

Finally Block

In addition to `try` and `catch`, Groovy also supports the `finally` block. The code inside the `finally` block always executes regardless of whether an exception was thrown or not. This feature is particularly useful for resource management, such as closing files or database connections.

Example: Using Finally Block

```groovy
def readFile(filePath) {
```

```
File file = new File(filePath) FileInputStream fis = null try
{
fis = new FileInputStream(file)
// Process the file
} catch (FileNotFoundException e) { println "File not
found: ${e.message}"
} finally { if (fis) {
fis.close()
}
}
}
```
` ` `

In this example, the `finally` block ensures that the file input stream is closed even if an exception occurs, preventing resource leakage.

Best Practices for Exception Handling

Catch Specific Exceptions: Always aim to catch the most specific exceptions first before catching more general ones. This ensures that each specific scenario is addressed accurately.

Avoid Swallowing Exceptions: Swallowing exceptions by leaving catch blocks empty can make debugging challenging. Always log or handle the exception appropriately.

Use Custom Exceptions: For complex applications,

consider creating custom exception classes to provide more context about an error encountered.

Keep Try Blocks Small: Try to limit the code inside `try` blocks. Keeping the code concise makes it easier to identify and handle exceptions.

Document Exception Behavior: Clearly document methods that can throw exceptions, including the types of exceptions and their potential causes, to inform other developers.

Understanding exceptions in Groovy is essential for building robust and reliable applications. By following the principles of throwing and catching exceptions effectively, developers can create code that manages errors gracefully, improving the overall user experience. Employing best practices ensures that exceptions are handled thoughtfully, leading to clearer, maintainable code. As you develop your applications in Groovy, remember that effective exception management is a hallmark of professional software development.

Using Try-Catch-Finally Blocks

In Groovy, a powerful and dynamic programming language that runs on the Java Virtual Machine (JVM), handling exceptions is similar to Java but has its own flair and simplifications. This chapter delves into the use of try-catch-finally blocks in Groovy, offering you the tools to gracefully manage errors in your applications.

1. Understanding Errors and Exceptions

In any programming language, errors are inevitable. These errors can occur due to a variety of reasons such as invalid input, unavailable resources, or logic mistakes. In Groovy, like in Java, there are two main types of errors: Checked and Unchecked Exceptions.

Checked Exceptions: These are exceptions that must be declared in a method or constructor's throws clause if they can be thrown during the execution of that method. Common examples include `IOException` and `SQLException`.

Unchecked Exceptions: These do not need to be explicitly caught or declared. They can occur at runtime, such as `NullPointerException` or `ArrayIndexOutOfBoundsException`.

Groovy also simplifies handling these exceptions because it does not require developers to declare checked exceptions, allowing for more concise and readable code.

2. Introduction to Try-Catch-Finally

In Groovy, exceptions are managed using the try-catch-finally construct. This control flow structure allows you to write code that can recover from errors or perform certain actions no matter what happens in the try block.

2.1 The Structure

The syntax for using try-catch-finally in Groovy is as follows:

```groovy try {
// Code that might throw an exception
```

```
} catch (ExceptionType e) {
// Handle the exception
} finally {
// Code that will always execute
}
```

2.2 Explanation of Components

try Block: Contains the code that may potentially throw an exception. If an exception occurs, control is transferred to the catch block.

catch Block: This block is used to handle specific types of exceptions. You can have multiple catch blocks for different exception types. If the exception type matches, the corresponding catch block is executed.

finally Block: The code within this block always executes after the try and catch blocks, regardless of whether an exception was thrown or not. This is an ideal place for cleanup actions, such as closing resources.

3. Basic Example

Let's start with a simple example that demonstrates the try-catch-finally structure in Groovy:

```groovy
def divideNumbers(int numerator, int denominator) { try
{
```

```
return numerator / denominator
} catch (ArithmeticException e) {
println "Error: Division by zero is not allowed." return null
} finally {
println "Division operation completed."
}
}
def result = divideNumbers(10, 0) // This will trigger the exception println "Result: ${result}"
```

Output:
```

Error: Division by zero is not allowed. Division operation completed.
Result: null
```

In this example, the attempt to divide by zero triggers an `ArithmeticException`, which is caught and handled in the catch block. The finally block executes regardless of the outcome, ensuring that the operation completes correctly from a program flow perspective.

4. Multiple Catch Blocks

You may want to handle different types of exceptions in various ways. This can be achieved by using multiple catch blocks. The Groovy example below illustrates this:

```groovy
```

```
def readFile(String filePath) { try {
new File(filePath).text // This can throw an IOException
} catch (FileNotFoundException e) {
println "Error: File not found - ${e.message}"
} catch (IOException e) {
println "Error: Unable to read file - ${e.message}"
} finally {
println "File read operation attempted."
}
}

readFile("nonexistent_file.txt")
```

Output:
```

Error: File not found - nonexistent_file.txt (No such file or directory) File read operation attempted.
```

In this example, specific exceptions are caught separately, allowing for tailored error messages. ## 5. Best Practices

Catch Specific Exceptions: Always favor catching specific exceptions instead of a generic Exception object to ensure you are handling only the expected errors.

Clean Up Resources: Use the finally block or, better yet, try-with-resources (if applicable) to manage resources like file handles or database connections.

Log Exceptions: Consider logging exceptions for debugging purposes, especially in production environments.

Avoid Empty Catch Blocks: Never leave a catch block empty. Even if you don't need to handle the exception, logging it helps in diagnosing issues later.

Understanding and properly utilizing try-catch-finally blocks in Groovy is pivotal for robust error handling and application stability. With Groovy's intuitive syntax and flexibility, managing exceptions becomes a straightforward task, allowing developers to focus on building great applications. By following best practices and structuring error handling appropriately, you can create resilient applications that handle unexpected conditions gracefully.

Chapter 10: File I/O Operations

File Input/Output (I/O) operations are fundamental tasks that every programmer encounters. In Groovy, a versatile and dynamic language built on the Java platform, handling file I/O is not only efficient but also straightforward. This chapter delves into the methods and classes available in Groovy for reading from and writing to files, along with practical examples to illustrate these operations.

10.1 Introduction to File I/O in Groovy

Groovy enhances the traditional Java file I/O operations with a more concise and expressive syntax. At the core of its file handling capabilities are several powerful classes from the `java.io` package, complemented by Groovy's own `groovy.io.FileType` and `groovy.io.FileSystem` built-ins.

Understanding file I/O is crucial because it allows your applications to persist data, read configurations, process logs, and handle user-generated content. Whether you're working with text files, binary files, or even XML and JSON formats, Groovy provides the tools needed to manage these files with ease.

10.2 Setting Up Groovy for File I/O

Before diving into file operations, ensure that you have Groovy installed and set up properly on your system. You can write and execute Groovy scripts either through the command line or integrated development environments (IDEs) like IntelliJ IDEA or Eclipse with the Groovy plugin installed.

Creating a Simple Groovy Script

Let's begin with a basic Groovy script. Create a new Groovy file named `FileIOExample.groovy` in your working directory.

10.3 Reading from Files

Reading from files in Groovy is simplified using the `File` class. Here's how to read the contents of a text file.

10.3.1 Using `File.text`

The easiest way to read a file's contents into a string is to use the `text` property of the `File` class.

```groovy
def file = new File('example.txt') def content = file.text

println "File Content: $content"
```

10.3.2 Using `File.eachLine`

For larger files, it's often more efficient to read the file line by line. The `eachLine` method allows you to process each line individually.

```groovy
def file = new File('example.txt') file.eachLine { line, number ->

println "$number: $line"

}
```

10.3.3 Using `File.readLines`

If you need to work with the lines as a list, you can use `readLines()` method.

```groovy
def lines = file.readLines() lines.each { line ->
println line
}
```

10.4 Writing to Files

Just as reading can be easily achieved, Groovy also makes writing to files straightforward. ### 10.4.1 Using `File.write`

To write text to a file, you can use the `write` method. If the file already exists, this method will overwrite it.

```groovy
def file = new File('output.txt') file.write("Hello, World!\nThis is a test file.")
```

10.4.2 Using `File.append`

If you want to append content to an existing file without overwriting it, the `append` method is your go-to option.

```groovy
file.append("Adding a new line to the file.\n")
```

10.5 Advanced File I/O Operations

Now that you've mastered the basics, let's explore some advanced file I/O operations that Groovy supports. ### 10.5.1 Working with Directories

You can also perform operations on directories, such as listing files or filtering them based on certain criteria.

```groovy
def dir = new File('path/to/directory') dir.eachFile { file ->
println file.name
}

dir.eachFileMatch(~/.txt/) { file -> println "Text File: ${file.name}"
}

```

10.5.2 File Copying and Deleting

Groovy provides simple methods to copy and delete files, allowing you to manage file systems effectively.

```groovy
File source = new File('source.txt')
File destination = new File('copy_of_source.txt')
// Copying a file source.withInputStream { input ->
destination.withOutputStream { output -> output << input
}
}
// Deleting a file destination.delete()
```

10.6 Handling Exceptions

When dealing with file I/O, it's important to handle potential exceptions properly. This can include scenarios such as the file not being found, lack of permissions, or being unable to read/write to the file.

```groovy
try {

def file = new File('nonexistent.txt') def content = file.text

} catch (FileNotFoundException e) { println "File not found: ${e.message}"

} catch (IOException e) {

println "An I/O error occurred: ${e.message}"

}
```

In this chapter, we explored the various file I/O operations available in Groovy, from basic reading and writing to more advanced directory management and exception handling. Groovy's syntactic sugar makes file handling straightforward and user-friendly, allowing you to focus on building your applications rather than struggling with verbose syntax.

As we move on to the next chapter, remember that mastering file I/O operations is crucial for efficient data management and for building robust applications that can handle persistent state with ease.

Reading from Files

One of its many strengths is its ease of handling input/output operations, especially when it comes to file handling. Reading from files in Groovy is straightforward, allowing developers to easily interact with text files, CSVs, JSON, and more. In this chapter, we will explore various ways to read from files in Groovy, focusing on practical examples that will help you become proficient in file manipulation.

1. Getting Started with File Handling

Before jumping into reading files, let's ensure you have a basic understanding of how to work with the `File` class in Groovy. The `File` class is part of the `java.io` package, which Groovy wraps around, offering added convenience through its Dynamic capabilities.

Here's how to create a `File` object in Groovy:

```groovy
def file = new File('path/to/your/file.txt')
```

2. Reading Text Files ### 2.1 Using `readLines()`

The simplest way to read a text file line-by-line in Groovy is by using the `readLines()` method:

```groovy
def file = new File('path/to/your/file.txt') def lines = file.readLines()

lines.each { line -> println line

}
```

```
```

In this example, `readLines()` reads the entire file and returns a list of strings, with each string representing a line in the file.

2.2 Using `getText()`

If you want to read the entire content of the file as a single string, you can use the `getText()` method:

```groovy
def file = new File('path/to/your/file.txt') def content = file.text

println content
```
```

This method is particularly useful when working with smaller files where reading the whole content at once is manageable.

### 2.3 Reading with BufferedReader

For more advanced reading scenarios, such as processing large files efficiently, you might want to use

`BufferedReader`. Here's an example:

```groovy
def file = new File('path/to/your/file.txt') file.withReader {
reader ->

String line

while ((line = reader.readLine()) != null) { println line

}

}
```
```

```
` ` `
```

The `withReader` method ensures that the `BufferedReader` is closed automatically after use, providing a clean and efficient way to read each line.

3. Handling Different File Formats

Beyond reading simple text files, Groovy can also handle other formats such as CSV or JSON, using libraries that facilitate these formats.

3.1 Reading CSV Files

To read CSV files easily, you can use libraries like OpenCSV or simply split the lines by commas. Here's an example using plain Groovy:

```groovy
def file = new File('path/to/your/file.csv') file.eachLine {
line ->

def fields = line.split(',')

println "Field 1: ${fields[0]}, Field 2: ${fields[1]}"

}
```

This approach reads each line of the CSV, splits the line by commas, and processes the fields accordingly. ### 3.2 Reading JSON Files

For JSON files, Groovy simplifies the process significantly with its built-in support for JSON parsing:

```groovy
import groovy.json.JsonSlurper
```

```groovy
def file = new File('path/to/your/file.json') def jsonSlurper
= new JsonSlurper()

def data = jsonSlurper.parse(file)

println data
```

The `JsonSlurper` converts the JSON content into a Groovy object, making it easy to work with complex data structures.

4. Error Handling

When reading from files, it is essential to handle exceptions to prevent your application from crashing. Utilize a `try-catch` block to manage potential errors:

```groovy
def file = new File('path/to/your/file.txt') try {

def content = file.text println content

} catch (IOException e) {

println "An error occurred: ${e.message}"

}
```

By implementing error handling, you can better manage situations such as missing files or access permissions issues.

In this chapter, we have covered the essential methods for reading from files in Groovy, including reading text files, handling different file formats like CSV and JSON, and implementing error handling mechanisms. Groovy's file handling capabilities make it a valuable tool for developers who need to work with data stored in various formats. As you continue to explore Groovy, you will find that its flexibility and ease of use significantly enhance your coding experience, especially in data processing scenarios.

Writing to Files

Writing to files is a fundamental task in any programming language, including Groovy. Whether you are logging application output, saving user data, or exporting reports, knowing how to manipulate files efficiently is indispensable. Groovy, with its simplified syntax and powerful features, makes it easy to interact with the file system. In this chapter, we will explore various ways to create, write to, and manipulate files in Groovy.

1. Introduction to File Handling in Groovy

Groovy leverages Java's file-handling functionalities, allowing you to work with files in a way that feels natural and intuitive. The `File` class, part of the Java standard library, is the cornerstone of file operations in Groovy. It provides methods to read from, write to, and manage files and directories.

1.1 Setting Up Your Environment

Before diving into file operations, ensure that you have Groovy installed and that you can run Groovy scripts. You can test this by writing a simple script that prints "Hello, World!" to the console.

```groovy
println "Hello, World!"
```

Save this as `hello.groovy` and run it from your command line using:

```bash
groovy hello.groovy
```

2. Creating and Writing to Files ### 2.1 The Basics of File Creation

To create a file in Groovy, you can instantiate a `File` object with the desired file path. If the file does not exist, you can create it using the `createNewFile()` method.

```groovy
def file = new File('output.txt') if (!file.exists()) {

file.createNewFile()

println "File created: ${file.name}"

} else {

println "File already exists."

}
```

2.2 Writing Text to Files

Writing text to files in Groovy can be accomplished in several ways. The most straightforward method is using the `write()` method of the `File` class.

159

```groovy
def file = new File('output.txt') file.write('Hello, Groovy!')
// Alternatively, you can append text file.append(' This is an additional line.')
```

2.3 Handling Exceptions

When dealing with file operations, it's crucial to handle exceptions, such as `IOException`. You can use a try-catch block to ensure your program can respond to errors gracefully.

```groovy
try {
def file = new File('output.txt') file.write('This text may be overwritten.')
} catch (IOException e) {
println "An error occurred: ${e.message}"
}
```

3. Writing Structured Data to Files

Groovy's ability to handle collections, maps, and other data structures makes it easy to write complex data to files. You can serialize data in formats like JSON or XML.

3.1 Writing JSON to a File

To write a simple map to a JSON file, you can make use of libraries like `groovy.json.JsonOutput`.

```groovy
```

```
import groovy.json.JsonOutput
def data = [
name: 'John Doe', age: 30,
city: 'San Francisco'
]
def     jsonFile     =     new     File('data.json')
jsonFile.write(JsonOutput.toJson(data))
```

3.2 Writing CSV Files

Another common format is CSV. Here's how you can write a list of data to a CSV file:

```groovy
def users = [
['Name', 'Age', 'City'],
['Alice', 28, 'New York'],
['Bob', 35, 'Los Angeles'],
['Charlie', 25, 'Chicago']


]
def csvFile = new File('users.csv') users.each { user ->
csvFile.append(user.join(', ') + '\n')
}
```

In this chapter, we explored the various methods to write to files in Groovy, from basic file creation to more complex

161

data writing scenarios like JSON and CSV formats. Groovy's concise syntax allows you to perform file operations efficiently while maintaining readability. As you continue to build your applications, mastering file handling will be a crucial skill that enhances your ability to manage data effectively.

Chapter 11: Working with Strings

Groovy builds on Java's already powerful string manipulation capabilities, adding its own enhancements that make working with strings not only easier but also more intuitive. This chapter delves into the many features Groovy provides for string manipulation, including creation, interpolation, methods, and handling of multiline strings.

11.1 String Creation

In Groovy, strings can be created using double quotes (`"`) or single quotes (`'`). The difference between the two is significant, especially when it comes to interpolation and escape sequences.

11.1.1 Single-Quoted Strings

Single-quoted strings are straightforward and treat everything literally except for the escape sequences. This means that special characters must be escaped if you want to include them.

```groovy
def singleQuoted = 'Hello, World!'

def escapedString = 'This is a single quote: \' and a backslash: \\' println(singleQuoted)    // Output: Hello, World!

println(escapedString)    // Output: This is a single quote: ' and a backslash: \
```

11.1.2 Double-Quoted Strings

Double-quoted strings allow for string interpolation, where you can include variables and expressions directly within the string.

```groovy
def name = "Alice"

def greeting = "Hello, ${name}!" println(greeting)     // Output: Hello, Alice!
```

11.1.3 GStrings

A special feature of Groovy is GString, which is a mutable string. It enables dynamic expression inclusion within a string. Besides basic variable interpolation, you can use more complex expressions.

```groovy
def age = 30

def message = "In 5 years, ${name} will be ${age + 5} years old." println(message)     // Output: In 5 years, Alice will be 35 years old.
```

11.2 String Methods

Groovy enhances Java's string methods with additional functionality. Some commonly used methods include:

11.2.1 Concatenation

You can concatenate strings easily using the `+` operator.

```groovy
def first = "Good"

def second = " Morning"
```

```
def combined = first + second
println(combined)  // Output: Good Morning
```

11.2.2 Common Methods

Groovy provides several methods that simplify string operations:

`size()`: Returns the length of a string.

`contains()`: Checks if a string contains a specified sequence of characters.

`toUpperCase()` & `toLowerCase()`: Converts the string to uppercase or lowercase.

`trim()`: Removes leading and trailing whitespace.

```groovy
def str = " Groovy Programming " println(str.size())   // Output: 19 println(str.contains("Groovy")) // Output: true

println(str.toUpperCase())   // Output:   GROOVY PROGRAMMING println(str.trim())   //   Output: Groovy Programming
```

11.2.3 Splitting and Joining

Strings can be split into arrays or lists using the `split()` method. Similarly, lists can be converted back to strings with the `join()` method.

```groovy
def sentence = "This is a Groovy chapter" def words = sentence.split(" ")
```

```groovy
println(words)    // Output: [This, is, a, Groovy, chapter]
def joined = words.join(" ")
println(joined)    // Output: This is a Groovy chapter
```

11.3 String Manipulation ### 11.3.1 Regular Expressions

Groovy's integration with regular expressions makes it easy to work with patterns in strings. You can use the `=~` operator for matching and `findAll()` for extracting substrings.

```groovy
def text = "The rain in Spain stays mainly in the plain." def pattern = ~/ain/
def matches = text.findAll(pattern)
println(matches)    // Output: [rain, Spain, plain]
```

11.3.2 String Replacement

The `replace()` method allows you to replace occurrences of a substring with another string.

```groovy
def original = "I love Groovy programming."
def replaced = original.replace("Groovy", "Java")
println(replaced)    // Output: I love Java programming.
```

```
```

11.3.3 Padding and Formatting

You can pad strings with spaces or other characters using the `padLeft()` and `padRight()` methods:

```groovy
def padded = "Groovy".padLeft(10, '*') println(padded)
    // Output: *****Groovy
```

11.4 Multiline Strings

Groovy supports multiline strings, allowing for clearer code formatting. You can achieve this using triple double quotes (`"""`) or triple single quotes (`'''`).

```groovy
def multilineString = """This is a multiline string

in Groovy.""" println(multilineString)
```

From string creation and interpolation to various methods and manipulations, Groovy enhances the ease of working with strings compared to traditional Java. Understanding these features is essential for effective Groovy programming, as strings form the backbone of most applications, dictating how we process and engage with text-based data. As you become more comfortable with these techniques, you'll find that string manipulation becomes a powerful tool in your Groovy toolkit.

String Manipulation Techniques

String manipulation is an essential task in software development, as strings often serve as primary data types for handling textual information. Whether you're working with user inputs, processing data from files, or generating dynamic content on the web, the ability to manipulate strings efficiently is crucial. Groovy, a powerful and versatile scripting language that runs on the Java Virtual Machine (JVM), provides a rich set of built-in features for string manipulation. This chapter aims to explore various string manipulation techniques in Groovy, covering basic operations, advanced methods, and practical examples.

1. Basic String Operations ### 1.1 String Creation

In Groovy, strings can be created using single quotes, double quotes, triple single quotes, or triple double quotes.

```groovy
def singleQuoteString = 'Hello, world!'
```

def doubleQuoteString = "Hello, ${name}!" def multilineString = '''This is a

multiline string.'''

```

### 1.2 String Concatenation

Concatenating strings in Groovy can be done using the `+` operator or by using string interpolation with double quotes.

```groovy
def firstName = "John" def lastName = "Doe"

```groovy
def fullName = firstName + ' ' + lastName // Using +

def greeting = "Hello, ${firstName} ${lastName}!" // Using interpolation
```

1.3 String Length and Accessing Characters

You can easily get the length of a string and access individual characters using index notation.

```groovy
def str = "Groovy"

def length = str.length() // 6 def firstChar = str[0] // 'G'
```

2. String Formatting ### 2.1 String Interpolation

Groovy supports string interpolation, allowing you to embed variables directly within string literals. This simplifies string formatting and enhances readability.

```groovy
def age = 30

def message = "I am ${age} years old."
```

2.2 sprintf Method

For more complex formatting needs, Groovy provides the `sprintf` method, which works similarly to the

`printf` function in C.

```groovy
def name = "Alice" def score = 95.568

def formattedString = sprintf("Name: %s, Score: %.2f",
```

name, score) // "Name: Alice, Score: 95.57"
```

## 3. Common String Manipulation Techniques ### 3.1 Trimming and Padding

You can trim whitespace from the beginning and end of a string using the `trim()` method. Groovy also provides padding techniques using `padLeft()` and `padRight()`.

```groovy
def originalString = "  Groovy  "

def trimmedString = originalString.trim() // "Groovy"

def paddedString = trimmedString.padLeft(10, ' ') // "    Groovy"
```

3.2 Splitting and Joining Strings

Splitting a string into an array of substrings can be achieved with the `split()` method, while joining an array into a single string is possible with the `join()` method.

```groovy
def commaSeparated = "apple,banana,cherry"

def fruits = commaSeparated.split(",") // ['apple', 'banana', 'cherry'] def joinedFruits = fruits.join(" | ") // "apple | banana | cherry"
```

3.3 Replacing Substrings

The `replace()` and `replaceAll()` methods allow you to replace occurrences of a substring within a string.
```

```groovy
def originalText = "The quick brown fox"

def replacedText = originalText.replace("quick", "slow")
// "The slow brown fox"

def                    regexReplacedText         =
originalText.replaceAll("[aeiou]", "*")  //  "Th*  q**ck
br*wn f*x"
```

3.4 Searching and Substring Extraction

To search for substrings, you can use methods like
`contains()`,   `indexOf()`,   and   `lastIndexOf()`.
Additionally, substring extraction can be performed with
the `substring()` method.

```groovy
def sentence = "Learning Groovy is fun"

def containsLearning = sentence.contains("Learning") //
true def firstIndex = sentence.indexOf("Groovy") // 9

def subStr = sentence.substring(0, 8) // "Learning"
```

4. Advanced Techniques ### 4.1 Regular Expressions

Groovy has powerful regex support, enabling complex
string pattern matching. The `==~` operator checks for
matches, while `findAll()` retrieves all matches.

```groovy
def text = "The rain in Spain"
```

171

```
def matches = text.findAll(/ain/) // ['ain', 'ain'] def
isMatch = text ==~ /.*rain.*/ // true
```
```
### 4.2 Using GString for Dynamic Content
```

Groovy's GStrings allow you to embed expressions and method calls directly within strings.

```groovy
def price = 99.99 def tax = 0.2

def invoiceMsg = "Total amount: \$$${(price * (1 +
tax)).round(2)}" // Total amount: $119.99
```

String manipulation in Groovy is efficient and intuitive, thanks to its expressive syntax and powerful built-in methods. From simple concatenation and trimming to advanced regular expression matching, Groovy provides developers with the tools necessary to handle textual data effectively. With these techniques in hand, you'll be well-equipped to manage strings in your Groovy applications, enhancing both functionality and readability. As you continue to explore Groovy, remember that mastering string manipulation will serve as a valuable foundation for your programming skills.

Regular Expressions

Regular expressions (regex) are a powerful tool for pattern matching and text processing. They allow developers to search, manipulate, and validate strings based on specific patterns. In Groovy, a language that seamlessly integrates with the Java platform, working with regular expressions is both straightforward and flexible. This chapter will delve into the fundamentals of using regular expressions in Groovy, along with practical examples to illustrate their applications.

1. Basics of Regular Expressions

Before we dive into Groovy-specific implementations, it's essential to understand what regular expressions are. A regex is a sequence of characters that defines a search pattern, primarily used for string matching. It can be used for various tasks, including:

Validating input formats (e.g., email addresses, phone numbers)

Searching for substrings within strings

Replacing parts of strings

Splitting strings into arrays based on specific delimiters

1.1 Syntax

Regular expressions consist of literals and special characters. Some common components include:

Literals: Normal characters, like `a`, `b`, `1`, `2`, which match themselves.

Metacharacters: Special characters with specific meanings, such as:

`.`: Matches any character except a newline.

`*`: Matches zero or more occurrences of the preceding element.

`+`: Matches one or more occurrences of the preceding element.

`?`: Matches zero or one occurrence of the preceding element.

`^`: Indicates the beginning of a string.

`$`: Indicates the end of a string.

`[ ]`: Matches any one character inside the brackets.

`\`: Escapes a metacharacter to treat it as a literal. ## 2. Using Regular Expressions in Groovy

Groovy makes working with regular expressions easy with its built-in support. You can use the pattern syntax and matcher capabilities directly in Groovy scripts or applications.

2.1 Defining a Regular Expression

In Groovy, regular expressions can be defined using the `/` delimiters or the `~` operator. Here are some examples:

```groovy
// Using slashes

def regex = /[a-zA-Z0-9]+@([a-zA-Z0-9]+\.)+[a-zA-Z]{2,}/

// Using the tilde operator

def regex2 = ~/^[0-9]{3}-[0-9]{2}-[0-9]{4}$/
```

2.2 Matching Strings

Once you've defined a regular expression, you can use the `.find()`, `.matches()`, or `.replaceAll()` methods to perform various operations:

174

```groovy
def emailRegex = /[a-zA-Z0-9]+@([a-zA-Z0-9]+\.)+[a-zA-Z]{2,}/ def email = "example@example.com"

// Check if the email matches the regex pattern if (email ==~ emailRegex) {

println("Valid email address")

} else {

println("Invalid email address")

}
```

2.3 Finding Matches

You can use the `.find()` method to search for the first occurrence of a pattern within a string:

```groovy
def text = "The price is $100.00." def priceRegex = /\$\d+\.\d{2}/

if (text =~ priceRegex) {

println("Price found: " + (text =~ priceRegex)[0])

}
```

2.4 Replacing Text

The `.replaceAll()` method allows you to replace all occurrences of a pattern in a string:

```groovy
def originalText = "The quick brown fox jumps over the
```

lazy dog." def modifiedText = originalText.replaceAll(/[aeiou]/, "*")

println(modifiedText) // "Th* q**ck br*wn f*x j*mps *v*r th* l*zy d*g."
```

### 2.5 Splitting Strings

To split a string based on a regular expression, you can utilize the `.split()` method:

```groovy
def csv = "apple,banana,cherry,date" def fruits = csv.split(/,\s*/)

println(fruits) // Outputs: [apple, banana, cherry, date]
```

3. Advanced Regex Features

Groovy also supports more advanced regex features, such as groups, lookaheads, and lookbehinds. ### 3.1 Groups

Using parentheses in a regex creates groups, which can be referenced later. This is particularly helpful for extracting specific parts of a match:

```groovy
def dateRegex = /(\d{2})\/(\d{2})\/(\d{4})/

def dateString = "This event happened on 15/04/2022." def matcher = dateString =~ dateRegex

if (matcher) {

println("Day: ${matcher[0][1]}, Month: ${matcher[0][2]}, Year: ${matcher[0][3]}")
```
```

```
}
```

3.2 Lookaheads and Lookbehinds

Lookaheads (`(?=...)`) and lookbehinds (`(?<=...)`) allow you to match a pattern based on what follows or precedes it without including those parts in the match.

Example of a lookahead:

```groovy
def lookaheadRegex = /\d(?=\s*dollars)/

def text = "The cost is 20 dollars and 15 dollars." def amounts = text.findAll(lookaheadRegex) println(amounts) // Outputs: [20, 15]
```

Regular expressions are an invaluable asset when working with strings in Groovy. Their versatility and power enable developers to handle various text processing tasks effectively and efficiently. Whether you're validating input, extracting data, or transforming strings, understanding regex in Groovy will enhance your capability as a programmer. As you become more familiar with regex, you'll discover new ways to leverage this powerful feature in your applications, making your code cleaner and more efficient.

Conclusion

Congratulations on reaching the end of "Groovy Programming for Beginners: Your First Steps into Coding"! You've taken an important step toward mastering a powerful and versatile programming language, and we hope this book has equipped you with the foundational knowledge and confidence to continue your coding journey.

Throughout this guide, we've explored the essential concepts of Groovy, from its syntax to its unique features that make it a favorite among developers. You've learned about Groovy's dynamic nature, how to work with data structures, and how to take advantage of its seamless integration with Java. Each chapter was designed to build upon the previous one, ensuring that you not only grasp the basics but also understand how to apply them in real-world scenarios.

As you close this book, remember that programming is not just about learning syntax and writing code; it's about problem-solving, creativity, and continuous growth. The tech landscape is ever-evolving, and staying curious is key to thriving in this field. Challenge yourself to take on new projects, participate in coding communities, and seek out new resources. The more you practice, the more proficient you'll become.

Don't hesitate to explore the rich ecosystem that surrounds Groovy, diving deeper into frameworks and tools that can bring your projects to life. Whether you're interested in web development, automation, or data processing, Groovy offers a plethora of opportunities to expand your skills.

Finally, remember that every expert was once a beginner. Embrace the learning process, celebrate your progress, and don't shy away from making mistakes—they're some of the best teachers. The coding world is at your fingertips, and we are excited to see where your newfound skills will take you.

Thank you for choosing this eBook to guide you on your programming journey. Keep coding, keep exploring, and welcome to the wonderful world of Groovy programming! Happy coding!

Biography

Davis is a passionate educator and tech enthusiast with a deep-rooted love for making complex concepts accessible to everyone. With years of experience in web development and crafting seamless web applications, Davis has mastered the art of simplifying Simon—one of the most intriguing and foundational topics in technology—making it approachable for beginners and seasoned developers alike.

Beyond the world of Simon and web development, Davis finds joy in exploring the elegance of Groovy programming, where creativity meets precision. Known for a relentless curiosity and a knack for solving problems, Davis is driven by a mission to empower others to unlock their potential through technology.

When not immersed in coding or teaching, Davis enjoys brainstorming innovative web app ideas, mentoring aspiring developers, and sharing insights through writing. This ebook is a reflection of Davis's dedication to building a bridge between learning and doing, inspiring readers to turn knowledge into impactful action.

Join Davis on this journey of discovery, and let's create something remarkable together!